AMONG WOLVES

AMONG WOLVES

DISCIPLE-MAKING IN THE CITY

DHATI LEWIS

B&H
PUBLISHING GROUP
NASHVILLE, TENNESSEE

Published by B&H Publishing Group
Nashville, Tennessee

Dewey Decimal Classification: 269.2
Subject Heading: EVANGELISTIC WORK \ DISCIPLESHIP \
JESUS CHRIST—TEACHINGS

1 2 3 4 5 6 7 8 • 21 20 19 18 17

*For my wife and kids who have helped me embody
these principles over the years. And for my Blueprint Family,
who embraced disciple-making as central for the local church.*

CONTENTS

ACKNOWLEDGMENTS

First, I would like to thank Jesus for sovereignly putting me in the right places at the right time. I know I am not the most gifted, most well-spoken, or the most talented. But, like Moses, He has taken the little I have to make much of Himself.

I would like to thank my lovely, beautiful wife, Angie. Everyone who knows us, knows that you are the real hero in our family. You are our backbone. And more than any other human, you have dared me and given me the freedom to find my identity in Christ and not in the culture.

I would also like to thank my kids, Trinity, Jade, Briaiah, Dhati Jr., Brayden, and Nathaniel. As a flawed man who often doesn't get things right, thanks for keeping me honest and never losing hope in me. You have taught me what true repentance looks like.

I want to thank my mom, Donna Lewis, for being in my corner since day one. Literally.

I would also like to thank my grandmother, Lillie Pruitt. Thank you for the sacrifices you made, raising ten grandchildren in times when our dads weren't around.

Keynon, you were there before the thought of being a pastor or serving in full-time ministry ever crossed our minds. Thanks for being my road-dog and trying to flesh out these principles before we could even call them principles.

I want to thank Stephanie for helping me get this content out and put it on paper.

I want to thank all the Blueprint Elders who have co-labored with me over the years. I would specifically like to thank John Onwuchekwa, Muche Ukegbu, James Roberson, Amisho Lewis, Sam Dulla, Mark McClendon, Jorge Mendoza, Chad Pritchard, and Rob Harden for the many late hours of wrestling through these principles and helping us implement them in our specific urban context.

I would like to thank the Blueprint Staff, both old and new, for putting up with multiple changes as we have worked to make disciple-making not *a* ministry of our church, but *the* ministry of our church. Thank you for all the years of endurance and sacrifice.

PREFACE

EVERY SUNDAY GROWING UP, I WATCHED MY FATHER PLAY football and proudly cheered him on. With a professional football player as a dad, I got to live the life few know—I had everything I could dream of as a child. I had a special talent that was similar to my father's talent in football, and I began using it at the age of five. As I grew older, football became my god, guiding me in all my decisions and feelings. I didn't smoke, I didn't drink, I didn't do anything that I perceived as detrimental to a long, healthy life of football. When football was good, I was good; but when football was bad, I was bad. Football was my idol.

After high school, some smaller colleges offered football scholarships to me, but I wanted to play football for a large school. I could not believe I wasn't recruited by a major Division 1 school. That's when I hit a low point in my life. I thought I could play for and attend a community college in California, in hopes that I might get a better offer to a major Division 1 college.

There was a void in my life. This became evident because when I thought about life beyond football—there wasn't much to think through. Without football, I was left with a sense of emptiness. I didn't know how to find my significance, because all I knew was tied up in that game. I went through a period of searching. I began to study Islam, Christianity, Buddhism, and other religions to try to find the truth. One day, my friend's mother bought me my first Bible. I started reading it the summer before my sophomore year of college, and I began attending a Christian church. I knew even though I was considered a "good guy," I was a lonely, arrogant, and self-centered man in need of help, in need of meaning, and in need of a new purpose for my life.

In my studies of religion, Christianity was the only religion that told me that I sinned and fell short of God's glory. Because of that sin, I was going to die and be judged. I realized God's standard was perfection, and I was definitely not perfect. Jesus died on the cross for my sin to satisfy God's wrath toward me because of my sin. There was nothing I could do to change that fact. I learned that I must accept the Lord by faith because a relationship with God was not something earned or deserved, but a gift. I learned Christ died on the cross for my sins and He was raised from the grave.

The Lord brought me to a point of repentance. At church, the way people "repented" was by going down to the altar and, at the time, I thought that was the only way to be saved. So one weekday, I decided that I would walk down the aisle and give my life to Christ. On the next Sunday, I transferred my trust to Christ as my Lord and Savior. That was in 1996.

In the early days after my conversion, I would hear people talk about David and Goliath and Samson and Delilah, and I would always wonder, "Who in the world are these people?"

I would go back to my dorm room and read the stories for hours on end. I felt so behind and so lost, but the desire to catch up is what actually ended up developing in me a love for God's Word. I began going to any and every Bible study I could find. I went to a different Bible study every day of the week with any campus ministry I could: FCA, Campus Crusade for Christ, Impact, and more. I wanted to learn my Word.

I also wanted my nonbelieving friends to learn about Christ. The problem came when I would invite them to these campus studies. Most times, they would not come because most of the studies were with predominantly white groups and they felt out of place. When they would come, they were unwilling to or just unable to make the cultural jump. They would give me excuses like "Man, it's not for me" or, "Come on, man. They play an acoustic guitar." I was left feeling helpless because I was learning about the Lord personally, but not affecting my culture.

It was when a guy asked if he could disciple me—even though I had no idea what that meant—that my life for the Lord began to take shape. I knew this man would teach me more about the Bible, so I agreed. He taught me what it meant to be proactive for the faith. Before that, my walk with the Lord was primarily a list of don'ts—don't go to the clubs, don't join the fraternity, don't drink, don't, don't, don't—but for the first time, I saw that God put us here with a purpose.

While I was beginning to catch the vision for the life God calls us to, I struggled to figure out how to communicate that vision to my friends. The campus ministries I was part of were mostly homogeneous. They did things a specific way with a specific style to reach a specific type of person. And ethnic minorities, the people I most connected with, didn't look like them, talk like them, or act like them. I saw an increasing need to minister to this group of third-culture kids.

They were a unique group of students who weren't raised in the church. They were raised by the streets in urban environments. They were raised on hip-hop, many from broken homes. At the same time, many of them were the first to make it out of the brokenness of their neighborhoods and families. The first to go to college. Not only were they minorities ethnically in a white majority culture, but they were also minorities in their own neighborhoods as the group that was the first to leave and pursue a college education.

After their lives were changed by the gospel, they carried a deep desire to do more than just reenact what they saw at church. They authentically wanted Christ in their context. Our vision was to have a campus ministry that created space for that. We didn't want a campus ministry to compete with other campus ministries. We wanted a campus ministry to compete with the clubs.

Out of a burden to create something accessible to invite my friends to, God laid it on my heart to do something that was both culturally relevant and doctrinally sound. I, along with a couple of other college students, started a ministry on campus. God gave it favor. So much so, that by the time I graduated, we had other colleges asking me to help them start ministries on their campuses. Once I graduated, I went on staff with Impact (which is a ministry of Campus Crusade for Christ International [CRU]) and helped start ministries all over Texas. I specifically helped start ministries that were culturally relevant and doctrinally sound—meeting people where they were.

What started as the burden of a hodge-podge band of brothers trying to compete with the clubs on our own college campus, grew into a more formal identity of pastoral leaders in the local church. The burden to help start a college ministry grew into a more specific burden to plant local churches. The burden has always been about helping people form authentic and purposeful community. As we grew, we saw the amazing benefits of moving from informal gatherings to formal ones. And we learned that God called that community in a formal way, the local church. So it only made sense for us to move toward fleshing out this same burden through church-planting.

During the past twenty-plus years of full-time ministry, I have often thought about the tension of delivering relevant truth in the urban context, i.e., *Among Wolves*. Blueprint Church (where I currently pastor) was founded to create a model that seeks to solve this tension by creating a church that is both culturally relevant and doctrinally sound, while fully present in the urban context. Blueprint would be a church that understands that disciple-making is not a ministry of the church, but it is *the* ministry of the church.

I have witnessed firsthand the power of the contextualization of the gospel in an urban context within the framework of disciple-making. I have seen how God can take a heart of stone and mold it into a heart devoted to Him. God did that in my life back in 1996, when I got involved with a group of young African-American college students who were excited about Jesus. And I believe Atlanta and other urban cities across the nation are full of men and women who are eager to know God in a way that makes sense to them.

God placed a burden on my heart, not just to plant a church in an area where it is needed, but He has placed on my heart a desire to start a movement. I wanted to plant a church that is known for its example, the blueprint that it creates; a church that provides a model for planting other healthy, culturally relevant, doctrinally sound churches. I want Blueprint not just to impact Atlanta, but to impact the world. My prayer is that my generation will be the last generation of urban practitioners forced to leave the urban context in order to be discipled. This is why I have written this book.

This book is about my story being consumed by God's story. This is not a book written for pastors. This book was written for anyone who has a burden to bring a tangible expression of the gospel into their neighborhood or network of relationships—a group of people who are willing to minister among wolves, in the most dense and diverse and difficult urban areas of our cities.

INTRODUCTION

AMERICAN EVANGELICALISM HAS BEEN BLINDSIDED.

Over the past two hundred years, our cities and our world have changed from rural to urban.[1] This has led to a much less homogeneous culture—neighbors no longer look like each other. In fact, sociologists now use two key words to describe the urban or city context—*density* and *diversity*.[2] This massive shift in population and increase in diversity has taken place with little impact or influence from the evangelical church. "Though 83 percent of New Yorkers are affiliated with some form of organized religion, only 4 percent identify themselves as evangelical, according to a recent study by the Values and Research Institute."[3]

This current reality reveals the need to establish new tangible expressions of the gospel within the context of the density and diversity of American cities. Ignoring the rapidly evolving city context is neither wise nor prudent. This new urban, the dense and diverse cities of America, is transforming and shaping our culture, society, and neighborhoods. And when I say *our*, I mean yours too—even if you live in the suburbs, or far outside a city, this reality affects you in ways you may not even realize. More than ever, urban culture influences every community, because culture flows out of dense and diverse places into iPhones and computers and televisions in the most remote places in the world.

I stay connected to New York, Los Angeles, and Atlanta every single day, unless I actively try to avoid it. Additionally, the simple fact is that the large majority of the millions of people who live in America live in the context of city. In this book, I desire to develop a strategy that will help indigenous disciple-making in two foundational ways: (1) embrace the density and diversity of the city context, and (2) create a culture of effective disciple-making as they establish new local families in the city.

We need indigenous disciple-makers to minister in a context that has changed beneath our feet. As American cities have rapidly evolved, our churches, in many cases, have not. Just as missionaries in a foreign field effectively reach a new culture by training indigenous leaders, we need to train indigenous leaders in the urban context.

In order to equip indigenous disciple-makers, I aim to help people ministering in cities all over the United States. However, primarily, this book will outline principles learned while ministering in the Old Fourth Ward, a city-center neighborhood in Atlanta, Georgia. The Old Fourth Ward, like many up-and-coming neighborhoods, is experiencing transition. Blueprint Church serves this historic neighborhood; I serve as the lead planter and pastor of this church. By definition, a blueprint is a plan/process that is used as a guide to start something new. The principles learned ministering in the Old Fourth Ward will help shape the principles applied in the book. Therefore, much of the research that undergirds this project will be based on ministry that has been taking place in the Old Fourth Ward.

Among Wolves will address the urbanization and globalization that is upon us. Urbanization will impact those living in the city, as well as those living in the suburbs and rural areas. Sociologists Gottdiener and Hutchinson explain, "At the beginning of the twenty-first century, more than 3 billion persons—about half of the world's population—lived in urban areas. By 2030, this number is expected to increase from 3 to more than 5 billion persons—some 60 percent of the total world population. This will be the first urban century in human history."[4] For the first time in human history, more people are living in or near a city than they are in rural or suburban areas.

With this reality, cities are becoming dense pockets of people—people from rural areas, people from the suburbs, people from around the globe, and people indigenous to the city. In some cases, urban sprawl is taking over areas now considered towns and suburbs. The same sociologists continue, "Most of the U.S. population is urban . . . fewer people each year live within the large central cities that were the population foci of the past. Instead, what we now call home is the expanding regions of urbanization that are associated with an ever-changing array of cities, towns, suburbs, and exurban areas."[5]

Among Wolves will take an in-depth look at the book of Matthew as we explore what doing ministry in the density and diversity of the city looks like. The growth of cities around the world has caused more cultural interaction and intersection in ways that have previously never happened. In Hong Kong and China, CNN reports, "Hip-hop is quickly becoming the most popular style of music across Asia, even eclipsing today's big rock acts."[6] The impact of globalization in our cities has affected all people groups. For example, inner-city kids can be seen riding skateboards while suburban/rural kids are following the hip-hop culture. According to *Vibe Magazine*, "The hip-hop-ization of skateboarding began with the skate-park boom of the late 1970s. . . . Skateboarding soon took root in urban streets, parking lots, schools, and public plazas."[7] The urban sprawl is forcing people groups and cultures to interact in ways previously unseen.

People connect with people who live in a similar reality to their own. Based on their research findings, the British Psychological Society argues that people like being around others who are similar to them because there is a greater chance to forge friendships or romance.[8] This study illustrates that meaning in life is determined by a shared list of codes, slangs, and/or mannerisms more so than even those who live in the same area or community. This detachment from a parish community or suburban enclave has put the individual at the center, rather than being held together by a geographic location. Culture is no longer geographically bound.

Cities are not only diverse culturally, but also socioeconomically. In urban settings, in a one-mile area, one can see extreme poverty intertwined with extreme wealth. This disparity can result in an "us" versus "them" mentality. People naturally form identities in groups according to their economic status. And these groups, living side by side, live in a state of conflict.

Often, one side tries to extinguish the community on the other side of the proverbial "railroad tracks":

> Stratification is often pictured as a pyramid of social standing. Those at the top control most of the society's resources; they also enjoy the most symbolic prestige and political influence. Those below are the most numerous and have the least power. The United States, despite an active ideology that preaches equality, in fact has the most unequal distribution of wealth of any industrialized nation (Philips, 1988). The top one percent of the population controls over 70 percent of the wealth, and the top 5 percent control over 90 percent.[9]

If indigenous disciple-makers are going to lead communities in these neighborhoods, they must be able to carefully navigate the dimensions of urbanization. This book seeks to help practitioners think critically and contextually, in order to have an effective gospel impact in the complexity of the current urban context.

OUR REALITY: UNITY IN GENTRIFYING CONTEXT

Historically, the church has not done any better than secular organizations when it comes to bringing unity among people from different cultures. Rev. Dr. Martin Luther King Jr. coined the statement years ago—"Sunday is the most segregated day of the week"—as he was speaking against the reality of the Jim Crow laws, the practice of segregating blacks in the US. Almost fifty years later, although Jim Crow has been abolished as the law of the land, people in society still have a long way to go in abolishing those kinds of laws in their hearts.

Recent events, at the time of writing this book, like those involving Alton Sterling or Philando Castile, and hate-filled statements against a people based on race like those of Donald Sterling, former owner of the Los Angeles Clippers, remind us that racism and prejudice are still a part of our culture and even in our hearts. The United States is still very fragile when dealing with some of the realities that come with urbanization. If this type of belief could be relegated to a small minority of people who are still stuck in the racism of the fifties and sixties, then the need for concern would be lessened. However, we are reminded by people who claim, "Let's make America great again," that these issues did not stay in the last century. That statement alone is a slap in the face to those who were under oppression during the "great" times to which they were referring. Although it may be painful to admit, if we are willing to be honest with ourselves and our society, it is not difficult to see that, no matter our ethnicity, we all are practicing bigots and demonstrate our prejudice in one way or another.[10]

The city of Atlanta's slogan, "A City Too Busy to Hate," is being put to the test due to gentrification. Ten to twenty years ago, urban was thought of primarily in terms of inner-city, homogeneous, black, and poor. Density and diversity were not descriptors used in regard to urban. The new dense and diverse urban is upon us because of gentrification. According to the *Oxford Dictionary, gentrification* is "the process of renovating and improving a house or a district so that it conforms to middle-class taste." Many people have their opinions about the pros and cons of gentrification. The reality is, gentrification is happening and is impacting our cities, for better or worse. I will summarize its impact with three key words—relocation, redevelopment, and reorientation.

First, *relocation* happens when the natives of a community are decentralized to a different community. (Usually this is done to make room for the new urban settlers.) Relocating causes a lot of anxiety in the community because it creates an "us" versus "them" mentality. Many times the native community fights to remain in their lifelong homes. On the other hand, the gentrified community fights for safety and increasing property values in the patch of community they now call home.

Second, relocation brings *redevelopment.* The middle to upper-middle class are accustomed to a certain standard of living. In pursuit of this, old homes are renovated, or entire communities are overhauled in order to erect bigger and grander homes than what once existed. These redevelopment endeavors are usually manifested in renovating homes, opening bars, clubs, and local trendy restaurants. Cities across America are facing the challenges of gentrification, and the Old Fourth Ward is no different.

Finally, *reorientation* happens when both the natives and the gentrified community learn how to live in harmony with one another. This concept is hard for most of us, mainly because of fear. It is not a fear of the unknown; it is fear of what we think can happen or what we have seen happen in the past. The fear for the native community is losing what they have called home for so many years or not being accepted by their new neighbors. The fear for the gentrified community is being physically harmed, their homes being broken into, or their newly acquired property being devalued. In the midst of this tension, the church can make a great impact on the community. Paul points to this reality in his letter to the Ephesians,

> For he himself is our peace, who has made us both
> one and has broken down in his flesh the dividing wall
> of hostility by abolishing the law of commandments

expressed in ordinances, that he might create in himself one new man in place of the two, so making peace, and might reconcile us both to God in one body through the cross, thereby killing the hostility. (Eph. 2:14–16)

We have the ability to show our neighbors how, in Christ, we are able to live in harmony, peace, and love in the midst of our brokenness and differences.

ATLANTA AS A CASE STUDY

The Old Fourth Ward garners national attention around gentrification for two reasons. First, the renovation of the old Sears building is a premier symbol of gentrification. In 2011, work began on this 2.1-million-square-foot building, formerly known as City Hall East, with desires of turning it into a live, work, play space called Ponce City Market. This renovation and vision draws people from Metro Atlanta and the United States to move into city life and into this neighborhood.

The second reason Atlanta is receiving so much attention around the topic of gentrification is the state of the Boulevard corridor. In the 1890s the Boulevard was described as "one of the most desirable residence streets in the city."[11] Dr. Martin Luther King Jr. lived off of Boulevard and influenced the Civil Rights Movement from this very street. Unfortunately, for the past several decades, Boulevard has been known as the center of crime and drug activity in Atlanta, as well as the highest concentration of Section 8 housing inside the perimeter of the city.[12]

While many people are attracted to the Old Fourth Ward because Ponce City Market, many are fighting for the socioeconomic betterment of the Bedford Pines community (the neighborhood with a majority of the Section 8 Housing). Some might credit Dr. King with igniting this flame for unity in the context of diversity, but this call to fight for unity started over two thousand years ago with Jesus commissioning His church to walk in a manner worthy of His name. *Among Wolves* will, hopefully, demonstrate how our churches can walk in unity in the midst of diversity.

THE AIMS OF THIS BOOK

The book was written to develop men and women within the urban context, and come alongside these practitioners to develop and defend a culture of disciple-making. To define the term, a *practitioner* is someone who is actively engaged with or "practicing" the issues at hand. If you live in a community with people who are different from you, then *you* are a practitioner! As the pastor of a church in the heart of an urban context, I have felt these challenges of doing ministry. Even in the midst of the challenges and joys, we remain committed to being an answer to the prayer of Matthew 9:37–38, when Jesus called His disciples to pray to the Lord of the harvest to send out more laborers.

The aims of *Among Wolves* are four-fold:

1. **Gospel-Centered:** *Among Wolves* aims to help practitioners develop a deeper devotion for the person and work of Christ through His Word. Throughout the book, we will allow the Gospel of Matthew to be our guide. This Gospel begins with the burden to establish God's tangible presence and ends with a confirmation of His presence and commission to continue the family's business.

2. **Local Church-Based:** *Among Wolves* aims to equip practitioners to make disciples within the context of the local church. Urban practitioners will develop an understanding of the identity of the church as family, allowing that to shape the activities of their local gathering. This can be applied in multiple contexts, such as Bible study groups, missional communities, and small groups—anywhere you seek to co-labor with other believers.

3. **Disciple-Making Oriented:** *Among Wolves* aims to equip the practitioner to see disciple-making, not as *a* ministry, but as *the* ministry of the local church.
4. **Urban-Focused:** *Among Wolves* aims to help the practitioner navigate through the beauty, complexity, density, and diversity that city-life brings.

BOOK OVERVIEW

The following is an overview of the eight movements of Matthew we will cover:

MOVEMENT 1: VISION FROM BURDEN

God's vision for your life is all about you and not about you at all. Understanding God's story, your personal story, the story of people around you, and the story of your city will help you discover what God is specifically asking of you.

MOVEMENT 2: ESTABLISHING FAMILY

The church is not like a family, it is a family in which God is our Father, Jesus is our elder brother, and we are brothers and sisters in Christ.

MOVEMENT 3: ENTERING THE MISSION

As we enter God's mission, God allows trials, temptations, and spiritual warfare as a means to prepare us for ministry, to instill in us greater discipline, and to draw us into deeper dependency on the Father.

MOVEMENT 4: FRAMING DISCIPLE-MAKING

Disciple-making is *our* capacity to lovingly transmit and embody the life of Jesus through the life of His followers. If it takes a village to raise a child, it takes a church to raise a

Christian. Disciple-making is not *a* ministry of the church, it is *the* ministry of the church.

MOVEMENT 5: A CALL TO DISCIPLE-MAKING: A CALL TO LABOR

God's presence is the fuel that empowers us to be fully committed to His call, to live fully as those sent to be sheep among wolves.

MOVEMENT 6: TRAINING FROM SERVICE

Laboring for the harvest is a critical part of our sanctification and growth, it moves us to compassion, reinforces our identity, reminds us of our inadequacy, compels us to pray, and it ultimately an act of obedience to our call to live radical, countercultural lives.

MOVEMENT 7: MOBILIZING CORPORATELY FOR MISSION

If we are to mobilize corporately for mission, we must hold to a compelling vision of Christ's call, move away from the anti-vision, resist uniformity, and move together in unity.

MOVEMENT 8: UNLEASHING DISCIPLE-MAKERS

In obedience to our Preeminent Christ, we pursue the Great Commission's call for us to make disciples in our jobs, our homes, and our neighborhoods—all with the goal of recapturing those arenas as vital gospel ground. We fulfill the Great Commandment while we do the Great Commission.

Our goal is simple: *We want to be the last generation forced to leave the urban context in search of solid discipleship.*

CHAPTER 1

MOVEMENT #1: VISION FROM BURDEN (DESCRIBED)

There are a lot of things you can do, but what is the one thing you must *do?*[13] *—Howard Hendricks*

I HAVE SIX CHILDREN AND I LOVE COACHING THEM ALL. I apparently coach all the time—I know this because my children tell me—whether they want me to or not.

I am not afraid to admit, I live vicariously through my kids when it comes to sports. I'm a natural coach—it's in my blood. I'm the dad who wakes his kids up at 6 a.m. in the morning for workouts to improve their game. I use sports in most analogies, I use sports as life lessons, and I use ambiguous sports phrases in everyday conversations like, "I am calling an audible." "Put on the full court press." "You have to give it 110 percent." I love sports and coaching, and it just comes out of me.

I will never forget the realization I had while coaching in a high school championship football game. I thought to myself, *I enjoy coaching, but this does not ultimately do it for me.* My desire to make disciples in the local church and my desire to help pastors make disciples in the local church is what scratches my itch. It is my deepest burden—a God-given burden. I can coach, and I can do it well. But I *must* make disciples, and I *must* help others do the same.

WHAT *MUST* YOU DO?

Each year, after the NFL season ends, I know two things will happen. A champion will emerge—they will own a title all year long; they will celebrate and brag and revel in their accomplishment. Second, all the other teams will evaluate themselves based on what made the champions successful. If the champions won because they were a defensive-minded team, the other teams will aim to improve their defense. If the champions won because the offensive attack was fast-paced, the other teams will work on becoming quicker on offense. And, if the champions won because they had an elite superstar, the other teams will strive to recruit an elite superstar. No matter the sport, owners, general managers, and coaches alike seem to think if they mimic the champions, they will get the same results as the champions.

We do the same in ministry. We live in a time where we watch our "champions" (the people who are in the places we want to be) and mimic them, hoping to get their results.

A story in the Bible describes this kind of situation. In 1 Samuel, the Israelites are at war with the Philistines. The Philistines have an undefeated warrior, Goliath, who has been the reason behind their victories in battle. The Israelites were trying to figure out how to beat this champion fighter. The Philistines' strategy was to take their top warrior and have him fight against Israel's top warrior. In the past, this strategy proved to be successful for the Philistines—it's what made them the reigning champions. But, God had a different plan. Instead of using Israel's top fighter, God used David, the shepherd kid. God used the one who wasn't even suited up for battle, the untrained one, the one who was only there because his dad had him on an errand for his brothers. While running his errand, David heard the offensive chants of the giant and was compelled to accept Goliath's challenge to fight—he even wondered why no one else was taking on the challenge. As David prepared for battle, King Saul offered him his personal armor. Instead of taking the untested gear, David chooses to fight with a simple slingshot and five smooth stones.

We all know how the story ends.

David ends up defeating Goliath and Israel defeats the Philistines. In this story, God demonstrates that success is not determined by a strategy. Instead, it is found in Him and in faithfulness to Him.

Think about it.

Have you ever wondered, what would have happened if David had taken Saul's armor? What if David tried to copy Israel's champion, King Saul? If he had put on Saul's armor and gone out to fight, he probably would not have been successful because his confidence would have been in Saul's armor. Instead, David chose to trust God's sovereignty and providence in his own life, choosing to fight in the way God uniquely gifted him.

This reality hits home for most of us. While seeking to make an impact in our neighborhoods, we often go to conferences, read books, and try to mimic our evangelical Christian champions. We look at great leaders such as Martin Luther King Jr., Francis Chan, Beth Moore, Matt Chandler, Priscila Shirer, and Tony Evans. We try to figure out all that makes them successful so we can copy it. Yet, we fail to realize that it is the sovereign providence and grace of God that makes them who they are. When we put our confidence in man-based strategies, we end up with Christian lives that are very similar to what we see in the NFL, we produce copy-cat Christianity. Whatever our heroes are doing, we do. Whatever our heroes read, we read. And our thought is that if we do what they are doing, we will experience the same successes they experience.

Is this how God accomplishes His will on earth as it is in heaven? Is this the process God calls us to as sheep among wolves? No, it's not. That's my argument. In this chapter we are going to explore the process that God uses to develop pathways for ministry in the lives of His people—*vision from burden*. We will pull from selected Scriptures and then land on the first of eight movements in the Gospel of Matthew: *Developing Vision from Burden*.

THE PROCESS OF DEVELOPING VISION FROM BURDEN

First, let's take a closer look at the process of developing *vision from burden*. If we are going to consider all the things we can do and then identify the things we must do—which we would call *vision from burden*—we have to be intimately aware of four stories: God's story, my story (your personal story), our story (the stories of the people God has placed around you), and finally the story of my city (the story of your context.)

GOD'S STORY

The first aspect of developing *vision from burden* is to realize that all vision originates from God. Henry and Richard Blackaby explain it well in their book *Spiritual Leadership: Moving People on to God's Agenda*:

> The world functions by vision because it does not know God. God's people live by revelation. Proverbs 29:18, although widely quoted, is also often misapplied. The popular translation is, "Where there is no vision, the people perish" (KJV). A more accurate translation of the Hebrew is: "Without divine revelation people run wild." There is a significant difference between revelation and vision. Vision is something people produce. Revelation is something people receive. God must reveal his will if leaders are to know it. The secular world rejects

God's will, so nonbelievers are left with one alternative—to protect their own vision. Christians are called to a totally different agenda, which is set by God alone. Throughout this book when the term *vision* is used, it will not connote the popular idea of a leader-generated goal or dream. Instead, vision will refer to what God has revealed and promised about the future. The visions driving spiritual leaders must originate from God.[14]

For Christian leaders, vision is something that doesn't come from human intuition. It comes from the heart and mind of God. A *vision from burden* begins with God's story. God's vision is for redemption that brings reconciliation. This redemption goes back to the fall of man and the declaration of the proto-evangelium found in Genesis 3:15, which simply means the first gospel. From the very beginning, God works to restore and reconcile man to Himself. God's story, the message of Scripture, the gospel itself is the good news that we are reconciled back to God.

Think about it.

After the first sin in Genesis 3, God kills an animal and covers Adam's flesh so he can come out of hiding and reconcile his relationship with his Creator. After the flood and the tower of Babel, God raises up Abraham to lead pathways for reconciliation through a chosen people. We see God's heart in Exodus 19:4 when He declares, "I bore you on eagles' wings and brought you to myself." The people of Israel were given a clear picture, all that had taken place—the ten plagues, the Ten Commandments, the flooding of the sea, the gnats and the darkness—all of it was because God wanted to be *with* His people. His desire is for nothing to keep us from relationship with Him.

The Ten Commandments are all about reconciliation of relationship. The first four are about restoring a love relationship with God. The last six are about restoring relationship with one another.

This pattern continues throughout Scripture. Did you know that twelve out of the seventeen prophets were written during the time of First and Second Kings? That is significant because God sends twelve men out twelve different times to tell His disobedient people, "Repent or I'm going to punish you." Twelve times he sends prophets with the same message, and twelve times the Israelites didn't listen. This all happens because God wants His people to be with Him, and when we choose sin and isolation, He brings about punishment and gives us over to our sinful, rebellious desires. The Old Testament ends in Malachi with God begging the people of Israel to return to Him. The response is disobedience and the result to their sin is four hundred years of silence. You see, God's story is one of redemption that brings reconciliation. In the New Testament, Paul captures this point in 2 Corinthians 5:14–21 when he writes,

> For the love of Christ controls us, because we have concluded this: that one has died for all, therefore all have died; and he died for all, that those who live might no longer live for themselves but for him who for their sake died and was raised. From now on, therefore, we regard no one according to the flesh. Even though we once regarded Christ according to the flesh, we regard him thus no longer. Therefore, if anyone is in Christ, he is a new creation. The old has passed away; behold, the new has come. All this is from God, who through Christ reconciled us to himself and gave us the ministry of reconciliation; that is, in Christ God was reconciling the world to himself, not counting their trespasses against them, and entrusting to us the message of reconciliation. Therefore, we are ambassadors for Christ, God making his appeal through us. We implore you on behalf of Christ, be reconciled to God. For our sake he made him to be sin who knew no sin, so that in him we might become the righteousness of God.

God has given us the ministry of reconciliation. We are now His ambassadors and the message we proclaim is "be reconciled." The work of an ambassador is not to re-create a different picture of the home country. It is simply to represent their home country within the foreign land. God called us to be His ambassadors in a foreign world with the goal of reconciling the world to Himself. God's heart longs for redemption that brings reconciliation. We see this manifestation in the person and work of Jesus Christ. That's the good news. Through the death and resurrection of Jesus Christ, the world has access to the Father. This is the story God has been writing since the very beginning.

If, as leaders, we do not understand God's story, we are in danger of crafting a vision that does not lead to God's desired outcomes. It's like a coach turning his players loose to start the season without teaching them how to run his offense. This is why we must study the story of God in order to understand the heart of God.

However, it's not enough for us to understand God's story. We must also know our own story.

MY STORY

If you know much about seminary or Bible college, you know about chapel service—a gathering of students, professors, and other faculty are forced (I mean . . . *encouraged*) to attend. What's interesting about chapel is that you have the opportunity to hear many gifted speakers, each with a unique burden from God. One day I got to listen to the Crown Financial guy. He had a passionate opener and taught about the 2,380 verses in the Bible on money and stewardship. He went on to say that the Bible is all about money and stewardship and God's heart is for us to steward our money well. He closed with a passionate statement like, "If your heart is not about being a good steward, then your heart is not after God's heart." Feeling convicted to the core, I left thinking about how to become a better steward of my money.

The next time I went to chapel, another powerful speaker taught about missions and declared, "Our God is a missionary God." He went on to explain how the Bible is full of missionary passages that display God's heart for missions. He closed with the passionate statement, "If your heart is not about missions, then your heart is not after God's heart." Feeling convicted to the core, I left thinking about how to become more missional.

The next day, another enthused speaker came to chapel and declared, "God's heart is for the widows and orphans." After giving verse after verse, he closed with the passionate statement, "If your heart is not for the widows and orphans, then your heart is not after God's heart."

After attending numerous chapel services, and hearing many more of these passionate speakers, I began to feel overwhelmed. I remember leaving chapel one day, and this revelation hit me. I thought, *Maybe God's heart* is *for all of those things. But maybe, just maybe, the capacity of God's heart is bigger than the capacity of my heart. And maybe I need to understand my smaller part in God's larger story.*

Our capacity cannot rival God's. This is why we must not only be intimately aware of God's story, but we must also understand God's providence in our lives and the way He writes His story *through* our personal stories.

Dr. Hannah, one of my professors at seminary, used to say, "If God calls you to be a farmer, do not stoop so low as to become a king." The question we have to ask ourselves is: In God's story, what is my part? And this is where we get the opportunity to discover God's unique providence in our lives. Let me illustrate it with my story.

In 2007, I had a life-shaping meeting with a man named John Bryson (JB). I had previously asked him to speak into my life. He knew me—he knew my heart for discipleship. He knew I had led a college ministry since I had gotten to the University of North Texas back in 1996. He knew my passion for the urban context. He knew that our college ministry was attracting students that few were reaching. He saw how this college minis-try morphed into a church plant over time. He also knew some-thing I was not aware of at the time: God had a bigger plan for my life than what I was aiming to accomplish. My aim was to stay in Denton, a small college town in Texas. My plan was to raise my family and disciple the students as they came onto the college campus. JB saw God using this season to prepare me but this was not the end destination. JB challenged—"Go! Start a church in any urban city and then you can be a hub for others to come, be discipled, and sent out to start more churches."

On December 15, 2007, I made a commitment with twenty-five others to move from Denton, Texas, to Atlanta, Georgia, to plant Blueprint Church. That initial conversation served as a catalyst for me to do some soul-searching with the Lord. I knew I had entrepreneurial passions and desires. I loved starting new things. But I didn't want church-planting to be something I just did on a whim.

So I began to look back over the last fifteen years of my life and ministry. I tried to recall all the ways I saw God's providence in my life. And from that, I developed a list of things I knew God had specifically burdened me to do; things that, no matter if I got paid or not, I *must* do because God wired me to do them.

As I looked at the list and considered Bryson's challenge, the details of my story became clearer. Seeing the specific things God burdened me with alongside His story served as the catalyst for me to leave Denton and move to Atlanta. If you are going to distinguish your part in God's story, you first have to do the work of understanding God's story—redemption that brings reconciliation through Jesus Christ—but you also must be intimately aware of your own story and His providence in the details of your life that forms your burdens and passions within your heart.

If, as leaders, we do not understand our personal story, we are in danger of being like David trying to wear Saul's armor. It's like being a NASCAR driver—being a billboard of everyone else's brand and losing God's unique fingerprint in our lives. This is why we must be a student of our own lives and experiences. Self-awareness is part of understanding the providence of God in our lives.

However, it's not enough for us to understand God's story and our personal story. We must also know *our* story (the stories of the people God places around you).

OUR STORY

In Colossians 1:15–20, Paul writes,

> He [Jesus] is the image of the invisible God, the first-born of all creation. For by him all things were created, in heaven and on earth, visible and invisible, whether thrones or dominions or rulers or authorities—all things were created through him and for him. And he is before all things, and in him all things hold together. And he is the head of the body, the church. He is the beginning, the firstborn from the dead, that in everything he might be preeminent. For in him all the fullness of God was pleased to dwell, and through him to reconcile to himself all things, whether on earth or in heaven, making peace by the blood of his cross.

In the person of Christ, we see both God's ideal man and man's ideal God. He is the only person to ever walk the earth with the fullness of God dwelling within Him. He has *all* the gifts of the Spirit. He is the full manifestation of God. For believers today, if we want to see a full expression of God tangibly on earth, we can't go to any one individual. We have to go to the church.

As Paul says in Ephesians 3:10, it is within the church that the manifold wisdom of God is made known. This body of Christ is where we see the importance of moving from God's story (His redemption and reconciliation through Jesus Christ) to my story (uncovering God's providence in my life). But we can't stop there. We must also consider "our story." This is where we recognize how we are to bring about the full manifestation of God's presence by linking up with individuals in our everyday lives—this is the *our*.

God surrounds us with other people whose stories intertwine with ours. God's primary vehicle for expressing His will and character is the local church—God's covenant family. He makes us interdependent with one another. Our stories combine to become a greater part of God's story.

We see this in Colossians where it starts with the fullness of God being pleased to dwell in Christ, who is the head. The image continues and goes on to explain how each of us are individual members of His body; unique in part, but wholly interdependent on one another. If we are going to develop *vision from burden,* we need to understand God's story, my story, and the stories of the people God has intertwined in our lives.

Most of us approach the Christian life in a very individualistic way. Our attitude says, "Everything Christ has done, I must do." That is mistaken and unhealthy.

When I came to know the Lord, I was living with a friend. My dad left our family when I was in middle school, and I started bouncing from family member to family member. In high school, a friend's parents took me in and cared for me. When I met the Lord, my friend's mom purchased a Bible for me. She encouraged me to ask the Lord where I should go to college. Four colleges recruited me, but I only took one college recruitment trip. When I got to the University of North Texas, I knew I was where God wanted me. At that time, I did not know why I needed to be there but I immediately canceled my other three visits and signed a letter of intent. It did not, however, take long before I found out why God wanted me there. On January 10, 1996, I met a guy named Art Hooker. He introduced me to my first Christian community. People who looked like me, had similar struggles as me, yet were gifted in different ways than me, surrounded me. As I got to know my newfound community, I realized this group of people genuinely loved the Lord.

The body of Christ surrounding me shared the same Lord but had different experiences—some came from single-parent homes, some from two-parent homes, some grew up in the church, and some were previously unchurched. *Our story* started to shape a desire to be a place of growth and stability for the next generation—we wanted to create an environment that was both culturally relevant, doctrinally sound, and missionally engaged. We wanted to create a place where we could invite our friends and they could experience God in an authentic way.

We saw this reality as bigger than one person! This was a God-sized vision, but God used me (and *my story*) to draw it out and used us (and *our story*) to apply it. We needed more people, people who were more gifted than me, and gifted in different ways than me, to pull off what God was doing. We got to know one another better as we spent time in prayer and ministering together on the campus. We learned one another's spiritual gifts, passions, personality types, and the experiences that informed our realities. We became more than a group of Christians hanging out together. We understood one another because we took the time to hear one another's stories and burdens. Part of developing a *vision from burden* for *your* life is asking the question: Who has God put around me to co-labor with? You cannot, and should not, do it alone!

If, as leaders, we do not understand the story of the people God has placed in our lives, then we are in danger of creating a ministry of lopsided mini-me's. It's like being a clone, where everyone looks like you, talks like you, and acts like you. This is why we must be aware of the story of others. Developing a God-sized *vision from burden* is going to take more than your gifts.

However, it still isn't enough for us to understand God's story, our personal story, and the stories of people God places around us. We must also know our city's story.

THE STORY OF MY CITY

Luke writes in Acts 17:26–27,

And he made from one man every nation of mankind to live on all the face of the earth, having determined allotted periods and the boundaries of their dwelling place, that they should seek God, and perhaps feel their way toward him and find him. Yet he is actually not far from each one of us.

Since God has determined allotted periods and boundaries for our lives—my story, our story, and our city's story are platforms for God to accomplish His work. To be aware of God's vision for our lives, we need to understand our context. When I talk about the story of your city, it can be as large as your whole city or as specific as your block.

A good friend of mine would say, "We need to seek to understand others before seeking to be understood." As evangelical Christians, we are often answering questions that people in our neighborhoods are not asking. We must get to know our cities.

If we don't know our city, if we don't know our context, we cannot provide holistic answers for the questions our neighbors are struggling to answer. Once we understand the problems and questions, we can answer appropriately. In general, the problems are either unbelief in Christ or idolatry of things that replace Christ as Lord in the hearts of the people. This can manifest itself in a city context in a variety of ways. But, we must seek to understand before being understood. Once we understand, we can then show them why Christ is better.

Earlier we identified Colossians 1:15–19 as a central passage in regards to understanding why we need our story. Verse 20 states "Christ's blood has made peace in ALL things" (emphasis added). Therefore, as we seek redemption that produces reconciliation we must seek it in all things. We must ask ourselves these questions. How do we see God wanting to redefine our city's story? How does He want to create His own story among your neighbors? How has He uniquely prepared you, in the "my story" part of the process, to step into the rhythms, problems, etc. of your city's story to bring the peace of Christ's blood into all things? We will talk about this in more detail later (in movement 6).

As we begin to understand our context more fully, we must wrestle through the process of contextualization. First, let me define what I mean when I call practitioners to contextualize the church in the city:

> Contextualizing the church in the city is the process of contextualizing the gospel through establishing biblical family in a particular neighborhood or city.

Some of us fear the term *contextualization* because we see the polarities it has brought in Christian circles. The word *contextualization* has been used in theological discourse to mean many different things—some ways are useful, some ways that are not—to many different people.

On one side, someone might talk about contextualization from the vantage point of becoming more like the world. We have some who feel like the church needs to be like the world in order to attract the world.

On the flip side, contextualization might mean being completely distinct from the world—don't look anything like the world. This posture is separatist in its approach. We might feel like if we make Christianity as boring as possible, as free from the world's look, feel, wisdom, and values, then we will have a clear understanding of when the Spirit is at work.

On one side we over-contextualize, but on the other side we under-contextualize. Neither extreme is very effective. We neither need to become like the world, nor neglectful of the world.

Contextualization is simply communicating in a way that the receiver can understand the message in his/her heart language, while maintaining the integrity of the content.

When considering contextualization, we need to maintain four values. First, the gospel *must* be contextualized. An un-contextualized gospel is not possible. As soon as I open my mouth and speak English to communicate the gospel to an American audience, I am engaged in contextualization. If you fly me out to China, I would either pray for the gift of tongues (Chinese, to be exact), or ask for an interpreter to communicate so the people can understand the message in their heart's language. The very language we choose to use is part of contextualization.

Obviously, this is not the only means of contextualization—there are countless examples. We must recognize that we will contextualize the gospel and the aim should be to do this both effectively and faithfully.

The second thing to consider is that even though the gospel must be contextualized, we do not put our confidence in our ability to contextualize. Paul writes in 1 Corinthians 9:19, "For though I am free from all, I have made myself a servant to all, that I might win more of them." He goes on to write,

To the Jews I became as a Jew, in order to win Jews. To those under the law I became as one under the law (though not being myself under the law) that I might win those under the law. To those outside the law I became as one outside the law (not being outside the law of God but under the law of Christ) that I might win those outside the law. To the weak I became weak, that I might win the weak. *I have become all things to all people, that by all means I might save some.* (1 Cor. 9:20–22, emphasis added)

Paul is saying that, even if we perfectly contextualize the gospel, only some will be saved. Paul knows that some plant, some water, but only God brings the increase (1 Cor. 3:6–7). Even though we must contextualize the gospel, we do not put our confidence in our ability to contextualize. We put our confidence in the power of God to draw all men to Himself.

Third, we must contextualize with a sense of urgency. A Christian hip-hop group called The Cross Movement released an album called *Human Emergency* several years back. I asked my friend, Duce, to explain what the "Human Emergency" is, and he told me a story about a bomb.

He asked me to imagine, "What if a bomb was ticking in your house, but no one knew where it was? You could hear the ticking noise in the kitchen, so you search all the cabinets and cupboards and finally look under the sink and find the bomb sitting there, ticking away. But, there's a catch. There's no timer. If there's no timer on the bomb, but you're sure it's a bomb, would you just casually go tell your family, 'Hey there's a bomb in my kitchen so maybe we should leave.' No! You would have a sense of urgency to get people out as soon as possible because you don't know when it might explode."

Our urgency should be equal to this, and this urgency should drive us toward a healthy contextualization of the gospel in our cities. Do you really believe that Christ is coming back? Does your church really believe that Jesus could come back at any moment? We don't have a timer to give us a countdown; we don't know the hour or the day. So we must operate with a desperate sense of urgency—the clock is ticking.

Finally, we have to understand that the goal of contextualization is reconciliation. We have already established this as a critical part of understanding God's story, but the emphasis goes beyond that. If we take a quick survey of the ministry of Paul, we see this truth expressed as part of his goal. In 1 Timothy 1:5 he writes, "But the goal of our instruction is love from a pure heart and a good conscience and a sincere faith" (NASB).

We see it again in the ministry of Christ when He says in John 13:35, "By this all people will know that you are my disciples, if you have love for one another." Paul states that God is reconciling the world to Himself and has given us the ministry of reconciliation (2 Cor. 5:18–20).

Just imagine, what if, as born-again believers, everything we did was done with that goal in mind. What if we truly sought to be God's conduits of grace to bring about His redemptive reconciliation? When we truly understand the context of the city in which we are ministering, leverage God's people who are co-laboring with us, recognize God's providence and work in our own stories, and view all of these things through the lens of God's story, something beautiful emerges. When we understand these four stories (God, my, our, city), we begin to develop *vision from burden*.

Remember, if we want to avoid a copy-and-paste Christianity, we must first do the work of taking ownership of our unique burden—unearthing what God has done and is doing by intentionally learning these four primary stories. Now let's turn and look at how these principles play out in the opening chapters in the book of Matthew through the life of Joseph.

CHAPTER 2

MOVEMENT #1: VISION FROM BURDEN (APPLIED)

HAS SOMEONE EVER WARNED YOU TO PROTECT YOUR MINISTRY vision at all cost? While somewhat true, we must also remember that this is not primarily our vision—it is God's vision.

Therefore, we must protect it as *God's* vision, and our unique role in developing our unique contribution. I believe every person should experience two things: living in a small town and flying on an airplane.

When you live in a small town, everyone knows your business, everyone's talking about you, and everyone knows what's going on in your life. You realize how your decisions impact other people. Living with a small-town mentality teaches us that we don't live our lives in a vacuum. One begins to see the importance of their life and they can own the fact that their life impacts others.

On the flip side, have you ever looked out the window as the plane is landing? You see thousands of cars that look like miniature toy Hot Wheels cars and those miniature houses from the board game Monopoly. And, when you see the landscape of the city and the movement of thousands of people, you realize how small you are—you are one in a billion. It makes you feel insignificant. The magnitude of life can be overwhelming. We can learn from both of these experiences: living in a small town and flying in an airplane. We can identify this same polarity in developing *vision from burden*. This is a key principle to recognize in developing *vision from burden*—the story is all about you (small town), but it's also not about you (airplane). What we see in Joseph's story is the same.

It is all about Joseph, but it's not about Joseph.

HOW GOD DEVELOPED A VISION FROM BURDEN IN THE LIFE OF JOSEPH

At times in Christian circles, we view stories in Scripture with a winner's circle mind-set. For example, in the story of David and Goliath, we identify with David. How many times have you heard sermons or read a book about facing your giants in the same way David did?

But there is a different reality. If we are in that story, we are most likely the scared soldiers afraid to fight Goliath, praying someone else would come fight for us. Some may find themselves more in Goliath's place, defying God and thinking they are invincible. The role of David, however, is more like the role of Christ: the hero, the conquering Savior.

In Matthew's Gospel, we see the opening chapter is all about Joseph but not about Joseph at all.

Let me explain. Have you ever considered why Joseph didn't get the information in the same way Mary did? With Mary, God directly told her she was going to have a child. An angel visited her, declared the message, and prepared her. She had time to process and think through the situation before discussing it with her fiancée. Joseph wasn't given a "pre-warning" from the Lord or told beforehand that Mary would conceive by the Holy Spirit. God intentionally used this process in Joseph to develop conviction about God's vision—a vision in which he would soon become a passive participant.

A "passive participant" is often described as someone who gives consent to perform an act that is often scandalous and/or illegal by virtue of their presence, even if they don't participate directly. In this case, I use "passive participant," to help show both passivity (understanding that it's not about you), but also the significance that, as a participant, you play a significant part (it's all about you). In this term, passive does not imply inactivity. Rather, it indicates the individual involved *does not bear the primary role*. This is something Matthew highlights in the opening chapters of his book.

First, Matthew explains this as God's story, but it is God's story in light of Joseph. He starts off with the lineage of Christ, and in the first seventeen verses he writes of the twenty-eight generations before Joseph—highlighting that this story is something conceived long before Joseph was alive. In Matthew 1:1, he opens the book with the statement, "The book of the genealogy of Jesus Christ, the son of David, the son of Abraham." From the beginning, Matthew is clear that this is a story all about God. It is about the coming of a Messiah, the birth of Jesus Christ. Matthew highlights it, but he highlights it in a way (unlike the other Synoptic Gospels) that uncovers the individual importance of Joseph.

Matthew's genealogy starts with David and ends with Joseph. He gives us a unique glimpse into the backstory of how Joseph received the news about Jesus' miraculous conception. In the midst of Joseph's doubt after hearing the news, Matthew writes to explain how Joseph was then commanded not only to marry Mary, but also to name his new child.

What we see is the process of God developing a *vision from burden* in the life of Joseph. A vision that is all about Joseph, yet not about Joseph at all. The lineage helps to display the key reminder that Joseph has a passive yet active role in this story— meaning that he is not the main character here. However, we

also see the magnitude of his role in the details that follow as
Joseph begins to take full ownership of the vision and call God
places on his life.

GOD'S STORY

Joseph is a righteous, outstanding man whose fiancée
approaches him to let him know she is pregnant. Think about
how Joseph would have received this news. Mary is pregnant
and he knows he had nothing to do with it, and she is claim-
ing the Holy Spirit did it. Joseph, being just, didn't want to be
a part of the perception this news would bring. He didn't want
any part of it. He had nothing to do with it. It wasn't his idea.
It just happened. Joseph makes plans to divorce her and call off
the wedding. But in the midst of his planning, Joseph is visited
by an angel. The angel says, "Joseph, son of David, do not fear
to take Mary as your wife, for that which is conceived in her is
from the Holy Spirit. She will bear a son, and you shall call his
name Jesus, for he will save his people from their sins" (Matt.
1:20–21). In the verses immediately following, Matthew goes on
to tell us, "All this took place to fulfill what the Lord had spoken
by the prophet: 'Behold, the virgin shall conceive and bear a son,
and they shall call his name Immanuel' which means, God with
us" (vv. 22–23). God's story is center stage here. Everything is
taking place so God can be with us. It's about Joseph but it's not
about Joseph. The emphasis is on Immanuel, God establishing
His presence *with* us.

MY STORY

Matthew clearly displays how the story goes from God's
story to my (Joseph's) story as Joseph fully embodies the role of
a passive participant. This wasn't his dream. It wasn't his vision.
He did not plan for his marriage to come about wrought in scandal. His plans were much different. Yet, he took on the scandal
of walking with a pregnant wife who was carrying a child that
had been supernaturally conceived by the Holy Spirit.

Joseph did this because he took full ownership of the burden and vision God placed within him. Ownership of his role in the story was not a passive act. He took on full responsibility and leadership for the manifestation of this vision. The final verse of the first chapter reads, "When Joseph woke from sleep, he did as the angel of the Lord commanded him: he took his wife, but knew her not until she had given birth to a son. And he called his name Jesus" (vv. 24–25). We see the process of God's story becoming clearer within Joseph's particular role.

In all of it, we see the tension between Joseph's secondary, passive role and the importance of his involvement. From the genealogy that leads to Joseph, to the conception that Joseph was not involved in, all the way to the angelic command for Joseph to marry Mary and name his new child—we see how this story is not about Joseph while simultaneously being all about Joseph. It displays the process God takes His people through to form ownership and responsibility for vision to be manifested in the lives of His people; people like Joseph, like you and me, passive participants in His scandal of grace.

OUR STORY

Even though Joseph had a significant role in the arrival of the Messiah, he wasn't the only player. Generations came before him—generations of men and women whose stories were knit together in the most beautiful way to pave the way for the Messiah. Joseph's story is intertwined with theirs; his does not exist without them. Mary's story is perhaps most intertwined with Joseph's. While God initially spoke to Mary and used her to tell Joseph of God's plan, after they were married, God primarily speaks to Joseph. Their stories and lives are dependent upon each other. All of their decisions had dramatic impacts on the life of the other. You cannot fully understand Joseph's story without understanding Mary's. As we look at all the different stories surrounding Joseph's story, we see how God used many different people to bring about this part of His story. This is *our* story.

THE STORY OF MY CITY

In Matthew 1, we see the process of Joseph receiving the vision and taking responsibility for it. The second chapter of Matthew shows us three other responses of how the news was received. First, we see the wise men worshipped Jesus (2:11). Second, we see how Herod sought to kill Him (2:13). Finally, from the sheer silence in their lack of action, we see the chief priests and scribes were indifferent to him (2:4). Many times, when developing *vision from burden* in our cities, these are the responses we receive. As we seek to plant churches and communities of believers to establish a tangible expression of Immanuel, these are the responses we get. Some will come as seekers and want to worship God with you. Some will make it their sole ambition to kill the idea and the vision. And most will simply be indifferent to it. The nuances of every community are different. So we must listen, pay attention, and learn our city's story.

CONCLUSION: CONNECTING TO OUR STORIES TODAY

What are the implications for us today in developing *visions from burden*? Many of us have great ideas and significant burdens for our context. We would love to see nothing more than the person and work of Jesus made manifest among us and our communities. But, for many of us, it is just an idea. While we have Christ in our lives, we yearn to see Him work in the lives of others who either seem like they are wholly indifferent to a movement or desperate to kill it. Over these next seven movements, we will look to the life of Jesus and see how He went from an idea, a vision of being with us, to a fully mobilized army. The movements begin by looking at a vision God spoke to Mary. Jesus wasn't here yet. The vision was literally birthed in her stomach. Her pregnancy is such a great illustration for the burdens that you and I feel. You know when you have that gut feeling that God is asking you to do something? That is a burden in its infancy, in its idealization stage. God took the vision He spoke to Mary and grew it until it had come to fruition through Jesus Christ and through His church. God has a plan to take your burdens, to give you a vision, and to bring that vision to fruition.

As practitioners wrestling with God's unique burden, we must do the work required in this first movement. If we *only* copy-and-paste what we see others doing, we will lack conviction. If what God has deposited in you is the *only* consideration, we will have many blind spots. If you *only* allow what's going on in the city to be the driver, you will lack integrity. We must wrestle to hold *all* of these stories in the proper tension in order to develop a *vision from burden*.

Let me close this chapter with a word that I hope will encourage you. In Genesis 1:3a, God said, "Let there be light." In Genesis 1:3b–4, Scripture states, "and there was light. And God saw that the light was good. And God separated the light from the darkness." One of the things we must come to grips with is that God is the only Being who can conceive an idea in His heart that comes to fruition in exactly the way He intended. For the rest of us, when we try to bring a new idea to fruition, it's either greater than we first conceived, or it fails to meet our expectations. But it's in that very process we see the depths of God's grace. Our inability should not lead us to depression; it should lead us to greater dependence and faith. What I want to encourage you to remember is that you are not in control of your ideas. But we serve a God who is. When it comes to developing *vision from burden*, some plant, some water, but only God brings the increase (1 Cor. 3:6–7).

As we move on in the remaining movements of this book, I pray we would be content with what God gives us—because what God gives is better than anything we could get on our own.

THE IMPLICATIONS OF DEVELOPING
VISION FROM BURDEN IN MY LIFE

When I was challenged to move away from Denton to plant a church, I began to seriously examine the story of my life and identify the things I knew I must do. The following is a list I developed. They are things that, no matter where I am or what my job is, I know these are the things I must do in order to live out God's call on my life.

My Burden (1): I have a burden to create an authentic and purposeful family.

My Story:

I grew up in a family of extroverts. We were a tight-knit family and I was very close with my brothers, cousins, and other relatives. Our family was always the life of the party no matter what neighborhood we moved to or whose house we were in. We were also a sports family who valued teamwork. Each of those components helped to develop in me an understanding of the importance of family.

My Burden (2): I have a burden to establish a strong disciple-making culture.

My Story:

I wasn't called to be a pastor so I could preach; I was called to be a pastor so I could make disciples. I didn't grow up in church. After I became a believer, I was surrounded by a lot of people who knew the Bible and were trying to live it out. They would often bring up stories of David and Goliath, Samson and Delilah, and I was like, "Who are they talking about?" Realizing how much I had to learn, I was propelled to start going to all different types of Bibles studies. Every night on campus I was at a different Bible study—Campus Crusade, Fellowship of Christian Athletes, Navigators, to name a few. You name it, I was there (at least once). Operating with the mentality of a football player, I felt like I needed to catch up, so I put myself in spiritual two-a-days. Night after night I would learn new things about the Bible and the Lord. And in that process I learned about evangelism and discipleship. They were brand-new terms to me. Yet, even my new Christian friends weren't talking about it. In my failed attempts to be discipled as a young believer, I knew God gave me a distinct burden to be the last generation that needed to leave the urban context in order to be discipled.

Burden (3): I am burdened to seek and celebrate unity within diversity.

My Story:

Being the son of a professional football player, there were times when our family had money, and there were times that we didn't. Like many professional athletes, a few years after my dad was cut, we were on welfare. I lived a life where I learned to be comfortable around the middle class and affluent, but I also learned to be comfortable around the poor and marginalized. I learned to be resourceful in my poverty and to be generous in my wealth. I learned viewpoints from lots of different people.

Often these viewpoints from evangelicals were completely different. I have been asked by friends in an African-American context, "How can you be a Christian and be a Republican?" And I've been asked by those in majority white, evangelical Christian contexts, "How can you be a Christian and be a Democrat?" I have seen the white culture grieve the verdict of OJ Simpson while the African-American culture simultaneously celebrated his acquittal. I've seen the polarities caused by Eric Garner and Trayvon Martin. I grew up and have spent most of my life in the middle of these two worlds. I've seen the polarization in our country that seems to be driven more by cultural predisposition than the gospel. It seems like on the heart level, even among Christians, we have no true unity.

God used the process of dating and marrying my wife as the catalyst to really expose this evil in my own heart. While I had no problem with interracial marriages for other people, I always thought I wanted to marry a black woman. It was my preference. I was the guy on campus that was all about racial reconciliation. I started an organization on campus focused on being brothers and sisters in Christ. But it was only a surface-level unity that I sought. I was cool as long as we were gathering together in the college meeting rooms, as long as we stayed shallow. But in the deepest recesses of my heart, I only wanted justice for blacks. Once I began to realize that I had this affection and attraction for this woman— this white woman—my heart was exposed.

I remember the first time I told Angie that I had an interest in her. In the best mac-daddy voice that I could muster, I said, "You're the type of woman I would want to marry . . . if you were black." All I knew to do was be honest with her. She had all the traits, all the skills, all the character that I wanted in a wife. But there was one problem. She was white.

I was wrestling with my own identity at the time. I was part of a white organization, going to a white church, and I was accused by my African-American friends as trying to propagate white Christianity. And now, liking a white girl was the catalyst for them to accuse me of being an Uncle Tom and a sellout. It got to the point where I asked some of my African-American friends, "Would you rather I marry a black nonbeliever, or a white believer?" Sad to say, many of my friends' answers were that I should marry a black nonbeliever. And they explained their answers by giving reasons why we needed to stay within our race. It was Angie, my soon-to-be wife, who helped me find my identity in Christ. I learned that I was living as a thermometer instead of a thermostat. I would go into each context and read the temperature of the context and do whatever I needed to in order to fit that culture. I would adjust to my surrounding instead of holding on to a firm identity in Christ.

Angie, on the other hand, was consistent. She had come to know the Lord in college and she was just solidly consistent. She was Angie among the white population and she was Angie among the black population. She didn't shift or try to prove anything to anyone—she was just Angie.

Not me—I struggled. The struggle I had is the struggle that I see today. Through our dating process, God brought me to this burden—a desire to seek and celebrate unity with diversity on a heart level.

Burden (4): I am burdened to establish a strong local church presence.

My Story

Early in my Christian life, I didn't like the church, partially because I didn't understand what the church was. I felt like there was a huge disconnect between the Bible and church. I kept wondering, *Why are we celebrating the pastor? Where is discipleship?* I didn't want to be part of the church.

But I kept going to church because of that annoying verse in Hebrews that tells us not to forsake the assembly of the body. If not for that verse, I would have stopped going altogether. I soon realized that while God calls us to make disciples, His primary vehicle to do this is His local church. I had to wrestle with the tension between what God says about the church and what I felt about it. If the church is Christ's bride, then I needed to be a part and help bring about health within the local church. Through this struggle, I saw the importance of establishing a *healthy* church as God's primary tool to bring about His redemption and reconciliation.

Burden (5): I am burdened to raise up strong male leadership.

My Story

A sociologist said, "If we want to solve the problem in America, we have to solve the problem in the city. If we want to solve the problem of the city, we have to solve the problem of the home in the city. If we want to solve the problem of the home in the city, we have to solve the problem of males in the homes in the city."[15] This sociologist recognizes the primary issue we need to address is the issue of the man, or the lack of male presence in the home. The reality is that 40 percent of Americans are born without a biological father in the home. In the African-American context, that number jumps to 70 and 80 percent. This is not just a problem; it is an epidemic.

I remember going to a Boys & Girls Club in East Atlanta, and asking the director how many kids he served on a weekly basis. He said they normally serve between two hundred and three hundred kids each week. Then I asked a follow-up question: "How many of those kids have both mom and dad in the home?" I remember he looked back at me and said, "What's that?" He was joking, but sadly serious at the same time. He continued, "Actually, there's probably about ten . . . actually I can give you more examples of two-women homes [referring to lesbians] raising up men." The raw facts of the situation grieved me and broke my heart. It was at that point I was burdened with the desperate need to effectively attack the issue of fatherlessness in our context.

Burden (6): I am burdened to be part of a long-term solution.

My Story

Growing up, I never had the gift of impressing others with my speech. I was the kid growing up who the girls would talk about and say, "You just have to get to know Dhati." And that's how I got girls to like me. Because I wasn't gifted with flashy speech, I learned that I needed to do the same thing with good character and be consistent over time in order to gain friends. Over time, I earned their trust.

And that's the same thing I see when establishing God's will in the church. A friend of mine, John Onwucheckwa, often gives others the encouragement, "Don't overestimate what you can do in one year. But, don't underestimate what you can do in five." To bring about lasting and significant change, I must be consistent over the long haul—do the same thing over and over regardless of who is looking.

Planting Blueprint Church could have involved doing lots of things. But these were the things I knew I had to do. And these were the things that served as the catalyst for me to leave Denton and move to Atlanta. If you are going to distinguish your part in God's story, you have to do the work of understanding God's story—redemption that brings about reconciliation through Jesus Christ—but you also must know your own story and His providence in the details of your life that forms these burdens and passions within your heart. Once you have a grasp of these two stories, it is much easier to connect with the stories of your community and city.

CHAPTER 3

MOVEMENT #2:
ESTABLISHING FAMILY

Don't seek to start a church; instead, aim to establish a family.

EARLY IN THE LIFE OF BLUEPRINT, I WATCHED A YOUTUBE documentary on the topic of gangs and how they operate in the city of Atlanta: *If the Streets of Atlanta Could Talk.*

What I learned was alarming.

- Criminal gang membership has increased 40 percent in the United States for kids under the age of eighteen.
- Homicide is the second leading cause of death for those between ten and twenty-four years old.
- The reason for the formation of gangs was bred out of the need for a sense of belonging.

In addition to the saddening statistics, regardless of how precise they may or may not be, I learned by watching this documentary, the video revealed why most young people join a gang—they feel alone, isolated, and hopeless. Gangs give these lonely individuals love, support, feedback, counsel, friendship, and money—a sense of family. One gang historian, Dr. Edwards, stated, "The overwhelming reason for kids joining street gangs is to meet the needs that were not fulfilled by their family, school, church, or community."[16] Each person in this video stated a variation of this reality—a longing for community and family. Community is something you are supposed to have in your family and it grows from there, but these gang members did not get this fundamental, foundational need met in their families.

The formation of gangs and all the activities this entails is not the only response to the need for belonging. Many times, even as believers, our insecurity leads us to similarly irrational choices. Our behavior may not be as overt and obvious as that of a gang member but the results are similar—disappointment, grief, heartache, and pain. The lack of being firmly rooted in the family of God causes us to make choices that harm us and place hardship on others. The church is God's response to our need for belonging. Teacher and trainer Chip Dodd once gave insight to a small group of us regarding the choices we make, "We will never say 'no' to what harms us until we have something healthy to say 'yes' to. Until there is a replacement, we will continue to accept second best."

Can I challenge you? In your desire to make disciples, please don't race to establish a nonprofit, or create a 501-c3, or even start a church.

Can I challenge you to establish a family?

I don't have to be in your context in order to know what the missing ingredient is to your broken city. Too often, what ends up happening is we seek to first establish infrastructure (our organization, church, etc.) before actually living on mission in our context. What we end up producing is an environment with a lot of overhead and very little impact. We answer questions that aren't being asked. We serve needs that aren't really needs. We employ tactics to reach people who aren't even in our neighborhood. In other words, rather than becoming students of our context, and forming our organization based on our conclusions, oftentimes we develop our organization and try to force our neighbors to fit into it.

It has been said, if you plant a church you are not guaranteed to make disciples, but if you make disciples you will plant a church. Or, as I prefer to say, *establish a family*.

MOVEMENT 2: ESTABLISHING FAMILY

The second significant movement in the book of Matthew is establishing family—manifesting the gospel in the family of God. Matthew 3 establishes God as our Father, Jesus as our elder brother, and believers as brothers and sisters in Christ. As brothers and sisters, we often struggle to connect with one another—especially when we come from diverse backgrounds. We have seen this play out over and over again at Blueprint Church. Many members have struggled to build community with people so different from them. It's hard to connect at a heart's level with a person they "know," let alone with someone they don't know. Matthew gives an answer to this serious and nagging question in the minds of so many people today.

My wife and I adopted our two youngest sons. They were in three separate homes before coming to live with us. You can imagine the despair each of the boys faced. At eighteen months and three years, they had never belonged. They had been cared for and provided for, but they never belonged. Brayden, four years post adoption, told my wife, "Mom, thanks for being my mom. Before you, I had a bunch of babysitters taking care of me, but never a family." He was seven years old when he said that. At a young age, he recognized something that each of us know deep down—we don't just need to be cared for, we need to belong.

In our journey to understand the nature of the church we often start off on the wrong foot. Michael Goheen observes,

Historically, the study of the church has occupied itself
with matters such as church order, sacraments, ministry,
and discipline. These concerns are important. But eccle-
siology is first about identity and self-understanding,
and only after these are established should the church
consider what it is to do and how it is to organize itself
to work out that calling.[17]

Goheen is correct. We need to begin with identity rather
than with activity.

We did this for our boys. We established identity: What does
it mean to be a Lewis? What does it mean to be a brother and
son in the Lewis family? Establishing this identity established
belonging, and ultimately family.

How do we arrive at a proper understanding of the church's
identity? Goheen gleans a helpful insight from William Shenk:
"The Bible does not offer a definition of the church or provide
us with a doctrinal basis for understanding it. Instead the Bible
relies on images and narrative to disclose the meaning of the
church."[18] So, one of the first places we should begin looking
when we try to formulate an understanding of the church are the
metaphors used to describe her.

Paul Minear has identified at least ninety-six metaphors for
the church in Scripture, such as army, bride, flock, body, temple,
royal priesthood, and chosen generation.[19] There is beauty and
wisdom in this for these metaphors paint a picture that make it
easy for anyone to grasp. They clearly point to what God desires
the church to be in the world.

THE IDENTITY OF THE CHURCH EXPLAINED

Of all the word pictures and metaphors used to describe
the church, one stands out above the rest: family. In fact, it is
so much of the essence of the church that it cannot even properly be called a *metaphor*. Metaphors describe what the church

is like or similar to—light, flock, field, building—but family is not metaphorical; it is a literal description of the phenomena we know as church.

*The church is not **like** family; it **is** family.*

God is literally our Father, Jesus is literally our elder brother, and we are literally brothers and sisters in Christ. Family is the primary way the early church identified themselves. This can be seen by the fact that the word *disciple*, so prevalent in the early part of the New Testament, disappears after the book of Acts. It is replaced by the term *brother* in the rest of the Bible. Family dominates the self-understanding of the early church. We could argue that this is because of Paul's letters, but it didn't come from Paul. It is deeply rooted in the revelation of Jesus Christ, the Son of God.

> Jesus came from Galilee to the Jordan to John, to be baptized by him. John would have prevented him, saying, "I need to be baptized by you, and do you come to me?" But Jesus answered him, "Let it be so now, for thus it is fitting for us to fulfill all righteousness." Then he consented. And when Jesus was baptized, immediately he went up from the water, and behold, the heavens were opened to him, and he saw the Spirit of God descending like a dove and coming to rest on him; and behold, a voice from heaven said, "This is my beloved Son, with whom I am well pleased." (Matt. 3:13–17)

Something of supreme significance is happening in these verses. Not only is God speaking—which is always significant— He is breaking four hundred years of silence. In the book of Malachi, the children of Israel are rebuked by God for serving and loving Him halfheartedly. The main issue seems to be that they failed to acknowledge God with the respect due a father:

> A son honors his father, and a servant his master.
> If then I am a father, where is my honor? (Mal. 1:6)

After God rebukes them and calls them to return to Him in Malachi, God goes silent. The next time God speaks is in the revelation of a Son that is fully pleasing to Him. There is much that can be said here but I want to focus on the fact that in the baptism of Jesus, God is revealed as Father.

The church is not like a family; it is family.

Our creeds and confessions focus on Trinitarian orthodoxy, but Matthew 3 emphasizes the revelation of God as family. What the revelation of Jesus Christ introduced into the world is that God is more than what we thought, namely that God is family. In our adoption as sons, we are brought into the experience of what God has always been. In church life we are usually more concerned about orthodox statements that express this reality than we are with living out the experience of family. My boys were not concerned about logistics—where they slept, when they ate—and they were not concerned with the fact that we called them our sons, they wanted to know that they were truly and completely *our sons*. God introduces Jesus into the world after four hundred years of silence and calls Him "Son."

When we consider the baptism of Jesus in Matthew 3, we usually think of it in terms of apologetic and theological categories. We note how the scene includes the Father who speaks from heaven; Jesus, the beloved Son of God; and the Spirit who descends on Jesus in the form of a dove. And in our apologetic agenda and zeal for theological precision we develop arguments for the Trinity. I understand, and wholeheartedly affirm, that this passage is important for apologetic and theological purposes. But I'm afraid that by swinging for orthodoxy we miss something precious and important for the life of the church. Namely, that the most emphatic theological reality presented to us in the baptism account is that God is revealed as family. God is a Father and Jesus is His Son and the Spirit affirms that bond of love. So we may be theologically precise in our Trinitarian understanding, but are our churches faithful in expressing the reality that God is family?

In his book *When the Church Was Family*, Joseph Hellerman writes of a time that he was made aware of this error in his own ministry. A friend of his came to pick him up at his office for a lunch appointment and, while he was waiting, picked up a brochure titled *What We Believe*, and began reading it. Afterward, the friend made a stinging evaluation. He said, "Joe, a person could read through your statement of faith and conclude that Christianity, as your church teaches and practices it, has everything to do with how an individual relates to God and absolutely nothing with how people relate to one another."[20] Hellerman later reflected, ". . . our church's doctrinal statement wholly ignores God's design for human relationships, a topic that occupies a great deal of the biblical record."[21] Paul consistently threads together the Fatherhood of God and believers' relationships with one another. He cannot think of God outside of His "Fatherness," and can't think of believers outside of their "brotherhood."

Our problem is semantics. When we say church, we don't think family. We have to understand that we are not simply planting a church, we are not starting a Bible study, we are not starting a 501-c3; *we are establishing a family.*

Theologians and philosophers may be concerned to speak of God as "the prime unmoved mover," as "pure actuality," or as "absolutely simple." But when the Bible speaks of God, it speaks of creation and redemption and ultimately the "Father of our Lord Jesus," and by our union with Him, the "Father of all who are in Christ." This understanding of God as Father and the church as family dominates the thinking of the New Testament, particularly the way Paul understands the church and ministry in the church.

Consider the purpose of Paul's Pastoral Epistle of 1 Timothy; he writes to Timothy so that "you [Timothy] may know how one ought to behave in the household of God . . ." (3:15). Consider

Paul's guidelines for pastoral ministry in 1 Timothy 5:1–2, "Do not rebuke an older man but encourage him as you would a father, younger men as brothers, older women as mothers, younger women as sisters, in all purity." Consider how the implications of the church as family played out in Paul's approach to ministry in Thessalonica:

The tenderness of a loving mother:

> But we were gentle among you, like a nursing mother taking care of her own children. So, being affectionately desirous of you, we were ready to share with you not only the gospel of God but also our own selves, because you had become very dear to us. (1 Thess. 2:7–8)

The steadfastness of a faithful father:

> For you remember, brothers, our labor and toil: we worked night and day, that we might not be a burden to any of you, while we proclaimed to you the gospel of God. You are witnesses, and God also, how holy and righteous and blameless was our conduct toward you believers. For you know how, like a father with his children, we exhorted each one of you and encouraged you and charged you to walk in a manner worthy of God, who calls you into his own kingdom and glory. (1 Thess. 2:9–12)

Paul had to say some tough fatherly things to the Thessalonians: "He who does not work, does not eat" (2 Thess. 3:10, author paraphrase). The concern is not only that we be orthodox Trinitarians but that we live out the experience of being the family of God. Yes, we must be clear about what we believe in, but our churches must be equally clear about being children of the Father.

THE CHURCH AS ORPHANAGE

The church is not like family; it is a family in which God is our Father, Jesus is our elder brother, and we are brothers and sisters in Christ.

God establishes family.

In Ephesians 1, the essence of the church's identity is that of adopted children. God the Father chooses and adopts us, God the Son redeems and unites us, and God the Spirit guarantees and seals us. As covenant members of your church, *be* a family. Operate as a family, not an orphanage. An orphanage is home to a bunch of undernourished, underserved children and a few overworked caregivers. The kids in an orphanage do not share responsibility for one another. Instead, two or three caregivers are responsible for the needs of everyone within the home. On the contrary, in a family, every member contributes. An orphanage is consumer based; there is a provider and a client. But a family is driven by responsibility, not activity. Family is a community that is responsible for one another and should be characterized by love and the fruit of the Spirit.

The Church as a Family	The Church as an Orphanage
Identity-based	Consumer-based
Everyone takes responsibility	A few caregivers take responsibility
Familial	Corporate
Organism	Organization
Needs healthy fathers	Needs generous and savvy businessmen

There are many metaphors to describe the church, but I would argue that the primary identifier used in the book of Matthew is that of family.

God breaks four hundred years of silence to introduce Himself as *Father*. Jesus then begins to preach about the kingdom of heaven saying, "Repent, for the kingdom of heaven is at hand. . . . Follow me, and I will make you fishers of men" (Matt. 4:17, 19). He goes on to address the different dynamics we experience in following Him. All throughout the book He references what we see most clearly in Matthew 10 when He says,

"Do not think that I have come to bring peace to the earth. I have not come to bring peace, but a sword. For I have come to set a man against his father, and a daughter against her mother, and a daughter-in-law against her mother-in-law. And a person's enemies will be those of his own household. Whoever loves father or mother more than me is not worthy of me, and whoever loves son or daughter more than me is not worthy of me. And whoever does not take his cross and follow me is not worthy of me. Whoever finds his life will lose it, and whoever loses his life for my sake will find it." (vv. 34–39)

The church is the family of God, redeemed by Jesus, empowered by the Holy Spirit to bear one another's burdens and manifest His love to the world.

The Gospel of Matthew is a hallmark book for clarifying this truth of the church as family. In the eight movements of Matthew, we will continue to see God's work fleshed out in the context of church. This movement is the backbone of all the movements. The gospel makes us family, this is an undeniable fact. If we miss this principle, we will find ourselves going *to* church instead of *being* the church. We have often stated that Christianity is not a religion but is relationship. I want to expand even that definition. Christianity is not just a relationship (singular) but relationships (plural). These relationships are comprised of our relationship with God, self, others, and creation.

FOUR RELATIONSHIPS

There are four main relationships we have in life: our relationship with God, with self, with others, and our relationship with creation.

First, our relationship with God is paramount—the other three flow from that relationship. The Westminster Shorter Catechism teaches that human beings' primary purpose is to glorify God and enjoy Him forever. This is our calling, the ultimate reason for which we were created. Our relationship with God is the foundation of who we are and what we do.

Next is our relationship with self. We, as humans, are uniquely created in the image of God and thus have inherent worth and dignity. We have value because we are His. We have worth and purpose because of the Lord. We have to accept ourselves the way the Lord accepts us.

Third, we have relationship with others. How boring would life be if we did not engage and care for others around us? God created us to live in loving relationship with one another. We are not islands and we are not meant to be loners! Our relationships with others teach us about ourselves. Our relationships with others allow us to experience love and laughter, frustration and passion.

Last, our final relationship is that with creation. The "cultural mandate" of Genesis 1:28–30 teaches that God created us to be stewards, people who understand, subdue, and manage the world that God has created in order to produce bounty.

What happens when these relationships go wrong? What happens when we do not have healthy views and relationships with God, our self, others, and creation? Hopelessness ensues. When we deny God's existence and authority, we become materialistic and worshippers of false gods and spirits (e.g., gangs, work, physical beauty and fitness, careers, food, lust, etc.). Once this happens, we begin to see ourselves as god, which eats away at our self-worth because we know we fall short of God's status. If we do not have a healthy view of self, we definitely will not have a healthy view of others. We will be self-centered, exploiting and abusing others for our gain. If we do not value God and other human beings, we will not show dignity to the creation God has given us to manage and care for. What a twisted web we weave when we deny the health of these relationships or when we are denied vital relationships during our childhood and young adult life.

FATHERS AND FATHER WOUNDS

One of the most treasured and important relationships we will ever have is with our fathers. Present or absent, good or bad, the father/son or father/daughter relationship is significant in shaping all of us. None of us were raised by a perfect father, which has left all of us wounded to one degree or another. Proverbs 17:6 reads, "Grandchildren are the crown of the aged, and the glory of children is their fathers." A wound, by definition, is any unresolved issue where a lack of closure adversely impacts and shapes the direction and dynamics of a person's life now. While a father wound is an ongoing emotional, social, spiritual deficit that is caused by the lack of a healthy relationship with dad that now must be overcome by other means.

Let me remind you of the statistics. In 1960, 11 percent of children grew up apart from their biological fathers. By 2012, that number had almost tripled to the point that one-third of children in the United States grew up without a biological father in the home.[22] In the same year, estimates showed that in the African-American community a staggering 64 percent of children grew up apart from their biological fathers.[23] Children growing up in father-absent homes are more likely to live in poverty, end up in prison, use drugs, be abused, be overweight, and drop out of school. In contrast, children with involved fathers are more likely to have better grades and verbal skills, are more confident, and are in better physical health.[24]

My family and I moved into the Old Fourth Ward (O4W) neighborhood of Atlanta two years ago. We put our children in the neighborhood schools and began investing in lives. In doing so, we met an amazing young man. I will call him John.

John is the baby of five boys and is being raised by a single mom. John comes home with us every day; he rides the bus home with my two daughters. My wife does homework with him, she cooks him dinner, and even buys him clothes and school supplies. One day, John and my wife had a great conversation. My wife was talking to all the kids about how the father is the institutor of identity—a dad is the one that helps you know who you are.

John said, "Well, how am I ever to know who I am? I do not have a dad." My wife asked him about this. John's father has been in prison since he was born; he has never met him. My wife asked how this made him feel. John responded with some very emotionally intelligent responses—"I am sad because I don't have someone to lead me. I am angry because he didn't think enough of me and my brothers to do right, so he ended up locked up." Angie encouraged and spoke life: "John, many people have your story. God is faithful with His mercies. You may not have the family dynamic you desire, but you have Dhati to look to as a guide. You have us as a family to lean on and to depend on as well as the family God has given in your brothers and mom. God is your Father. God is able to teach you, and He thinks very highly of you."

The absence of a father is hard to overcome. While we do not have to be dominated by our past, overcoming the implications of these wounds is difficult. Praise be to God, Jesus has overcome the wounds of this world, including father wounds! He has provided the means, through the church, to meet the greatest needs in our homes and our city—a need for security, a need for significance, and a need for hope. The unique Father-Son relationship Jesus has with the Father grants us confidence to draw near to Him. If Jesus is equal to God (John 5:16–18; 10:28–30), then He must know how to be a Father since God is our perfect Father. John 14:6–7 sums up Jesus' relationship with God the Father: "Jesus said to him, 'I am the way, and the truth, and the life. No one comes to the Father except through me. If you had known me, you would have known my Father also. From now on you do know him and have seen him.'"

The answer for how to overcome our father wounds is found in Hebrews 4:14, 16: "Since then we have a great high priest who has passed through the heavens, Jesus, the Son of God, let us hold fast our confession. . . . Let us then with confidence draw near to the throne of grace, that we may receive mercy and find grace to help in time of need." In order for us to see healing and wholeness in our lives, our homes, and our cities, we must see God as Father and know we have access to Him through His Son Jesus. The health of our relationships with our heavenly Father determines the health of our relationships with others. In the New Testament, we see God revealed as Abba Father. Abba reminds us of the intimacy we have with Him. While Father reminds us of His ultimate authority.

Romans 8:14–17 clearly shows us our relationship:

> For all who are led by the Spirit of God are sons of God. For you did not receive the spirit of slavery to fall back into fear, but you have received the Spirit of adoption as sons, by whom we cry, "Abba! Father!" The Spirit himself bears witness with our spirit that we are children of God, and if children, then heirs—heirs of God and fellow heirs with Christ, provided we suffer with him in order that we may also glorified with him.

God's grace alone, manifested by His love for us, is His vehicle for fathering us. We are in a new family, characterized by love, hope, and purpose. God's love gives us security, a new identity, and a new example for what family looks like. God's love gives us hope because we now have a relationship with Jesus (God incarnate). Finally, God's love gives us purpose because we have a new mission and focus in this life. Now that we know we have a Father who loves us deeply and pursues us passionately, we can begin the process of embracing our high calling to make disciples.

John the Baptist calls sinners to repent and be baptized. He understands he cannot take away sins, but he prepares the way for the One who will, Jesus Christ. Jesus' baptism was a big deal.

John paves the way for the Father to say what we all long to hear, "This is my Son, in whom I am well pleased."

CHAPTER 4

MOVEMENT #3: ENTERING THE MISSION

EVERYONE FACES TEMPTATION. MINISTRY CAN BE A VERY TRYING and emotional experience. You will be tempted to make poor decisions based on emotions. You will be tempted to circumvent the process of mission in the city.

As we were gearing up to plant Blueprint Church in Atlanta, my family and I moved to Little Rock, Arkansas, for ten months as a time of preparation. While there, our job was simply to prepare. This was designed to be a time of focus, support, and clarity.

However, as we were beginning this time, I received a call from my stepmother telling me that my father had taken himself to the hospital because he couldn't feel his right arm. Long story short, that issue was due to a malignant tumor that eventually took his life. I got that phone call in June and by September my dad, my hero, had passed away. My dad was a healthy person; he worked out regularly, ate healthy food, and took care of himself. The tumor seemed to come out of nowhere.

His health declined so rapidly. We received the news in June, the same month we moved to Little Rock, away from anyone we knew. We were alone, sad, scared, and, honestly, a little lost. It rocked the foundation of my faith and took me into a state of emotional turmoil and questioning. We had four babies at the time as well—my oldest was only five years old. I had to fly out to California alone to face family that was broken and didn't have the hope of the gospel to comfort them.

I was weak and so much was being asked of me. I was in a season where I was facing spiritual warfare and temptation. One of the questions I had during that time was, "Why does God allow temptations?" Even more than that, "Why does God allow temptations in times when you are intentionally seeking to do God's will?" As I have talked to people seeking to enter ministry, it seems like temptation always strikes as we are entering these life-shaping seasons. As a dear brother of mine was preparing to begin a church, he got a phone call that his older brother had been found dead (of natural causes) in his car. Another brother of mine, as he prepared to start a new ministry and church, found out that his mother was being taken to the hospital and was in a coma. Another family moved across the country to be a part of Blueprint only to find out that their father had a brain tumor and would soon pass away as well. While there is never a good time to be tempted, or to engage in intense spiritual warfare, it seems like it would be better *not* to go through it at the beginning of ministry. Wouldn't it be better if we could first get our footing? Wouldn't we be able to handle temptations better at that point?

The frequency of this type of warfare at the beginning of ministry cannot be a coincidence. So the question comes back: why does God allow temptation and struggle?

I wrestled with the Lord over this question. I was angry; I doubted. I wondered if God was real, if He was good, if He was looking out for my best interests. As I wrestled with these questions, I learned that He allows temptations like these to prepare us for greater discipline and dependency as we enter into His mission.

Sometimes temptations are not just in doubt. Sometimes we struggle with our own successes. We sin against the Lord with our pride, with our self-righteousness. We find ourselves arrogant and unteachable. We find ourselves competing for fame. We are tempted to prove the naysayers wrong. We are sucked into gossip and we fail in relational conflict. We are tempted with relationships with the opposite gender. It seems to come on full force.

Remember, Christ is sending us as sheep in the midst of wolves.

The wolves are hungry—they are ready to destroy. They are slick and they are crafty. In my eight years of ministry, three dear friends of mine—pastors and leaders—have "found" themselves in extramarital affairs. Maybe the care they offered to someone grew into affection. Maybe their position led to the idea that they were above rules and the need for barriers and accountability. Temptations are real regardless of the avenues. There is a certain vulnerability that comes with the call to submit to the Lord and lead His people. The question is, what do we do with that vulnerability?

One of my mentors, Dr. Crawford Lorrits, used to say, "We need to be careful with ministry because sometimes our gifts will take us to places that our character can't handle." In the midst of these times of temptation, it is imperative that we run boldly to the cross.

TEMPTATION IN THE TEXT

There are parallels to the temptations Jesus endured as He entered His earthly ministry. Consider how Jesus was tempted. As we look into the beginning of His ministry, we should be reminded of these things.

First, Jesus was led into temptation in the wilderness by the Spirit! This is a powerful reminder that in the midst of our trials,

God is not absent; He is actually up to something! He is trying to do a work within you in ways you can't even fathom.

Second, temptation is usually most effective in our most vulnerable times. Jesus was not exempt from that. He had been fasting for forty days and nights and He was hungry—putting Him in a more vulnerable place to be swayed by the enemy's schemes.

Third, we see that all the temptations Satan suggested were intended to bring immediate satisfaction. Satan was attacking Jesus at a vulnerable point. But, we see that as Christ engaged, He did not argue or try to reason with Satan. Instead, He hid behind the Word of God. Jesus was tempted three times, and three times, He responded from the same source.

Let's look more closely at the Scriptures to understand how Jesus dealt with these temptations. The first temptation of Christ comes in Matthew 4:3 when Satan gives the challenge, "If you are the Son of God, command these stones to become loaves of bread." After forty days of not eating, this was a real and powerful temptation. What was at stake here is whether Jesus would live controlled by fleshly desires or by spiritual priorities. Jesus responded to him by saying, "It is written, 'Man shall not live by bread alone'" (v. 4).

The second temptation we see is when Satan tells Jesus, "Throw yourself from the temple and God's angels will come and rescue you" (v. 6, author paraphrase). This temptation is powerful because it challenges Jesus' view of God. In essence, the enemy is telling Jesus, "Since You are doing God's will, why don't You act carelessly and see God come to work on Your behalf." Basically, he's saying, "Let's see if God comes to Your rescue."

The temptation here is to pursue the right thing in the wrong way and allow the pursuit to become idolatrous. It is presuming upon God by trying to force God to serve our agenda, trying to force God's hand to act. The thought that comes along with this is: "If I am trying to do my part, God, You need to do Your part." This can oftentimes be translated to: "Whatever

I do in this pursuit needs to be blessed by You." Jesus responded by saying, "'You shall not put the Lord your God to the test'" (Matt. 4:7).

In the third and final temptation, Satan says, "If you will worship me all authority will be yours" (vv. 8–9, author paraphrase). Here, Satan goes back to his old tricks. He offers Christ the likeness of God and the possession of all authority, glory, and power. This has been his method since Genesis. In the story of Adam and Eve, Satan challenged Adam and Eve and told them, "If you eat of that tree, you will become like God" (Gen. 3:5, author paraphrase). In the same way, the temptation in Matthew 4 was to believe that God was withholding power and glory from Jesus. Satan tempted Jesus by telling Him that he would provide what God had been withholding. There was nothing wrong with the offer because all authority belongs to Jesus. The problem was in the fine print: Jesus had to worship Satan in order to obtain it. Jesus would have to shift His allegiance. Satan appeals to the flesh and pride of life, tempting Jesus to seek power immediately. Jesus, once again, responds with the Words of Life, reminding Satan that, "You shall worship the Lord your God and him only shall you serve" (Matt. 4:10).

In each one of these temptations, Satan tried to circumvent the process God put in place. Through Jesus, God allowed us to see what it looks like to practice greater discipline and dependency on the Father. Hebrews 5:8 tells us that "Although he was a son, he learned obedience through what he suffered." In Matthew 3 Jesus is declared to be the Son of God, and in Matthew 4 He is thrust into the most trying time of His life up to this point. Sonship did not exempt Him from suffering temptation. Neither will our sonship exempt us from suffering and temptation. Like Jesus suffering, temptation will equip us for our ministry as well. It is often a part of God's plan and should not surprise us. Paul's words in Philippians remind us and encourage us in this: "It has been granted to you that for the sake of Christ you should not only believe in him but also suffer for his sake" (Phil. 1:29).

TEMPTATION ON GOD'S MISSION: MORE DISCIPLINED, MORE DEPENDENT

As missionaries entering God's mission, we will face temptations similar to the ones Jesus faced. The first one we see is that we will be tempted in the area of provision. I remember when I first felt the Lord calling me to move from Denton to Atlanta. I had a great job and a steady income. When Angie and I first got married, I was making $800 a month and was raising support. At this point, I was on staff at a church, doing exactly what I wanted to do with college students, making $40K a year and living in a nice neighborhood within walking distance from our church. The kids would go to a good school, the church building was given to us, the bills for the building were paid. We were in a good spot. We were tempted to stay.

God was clear in His direction so we left Denton. We left and moved into a little apartment, made considerably less money, and left family and friends and all that we had known for the past twelve years. And then my dad passed. I was tempted to run to comfort, security, and material provisions instead of fully trusting the Lord.

Another similarity to Jesus' temptations is that we will be tempted to presume upon God. I see this in missionaries all the time as we say, "Lord, I am going to reorganize and reorient my life in order to do this. Therefore, You *must* provide for me." It's the person who just went to seminary and spent the last four years getting their degree and now feels entitled to make careless financial decisions in order to do what they have just been trained to do. It's the person who quits their job before having any income and expects God to meet those needs. Oftentimes, I see people with a sincere desire to do God's will act carelessly and expect God to meet them in their foolish decision. Many times we are tempted to presume upon God to bless our reckless choices. The statement that comes alongside this is: "I'm doing this for God, so it's okay for me to make reckless choices/decisions."

The final temptation I have seen as people enter the mission is the temptation to usurp power and glory. In a Christianity that's characterized by conferences, concerts, and church services, we are often seeking platforms and stages that will give us power and fame. Oftentimes the missionary can subtly shift their focus from, "Thy will be done," to "My will be done." And they begin to do things based not upon the advancement of the kingdom, but based on whether or not it will advance their platform. The statement that usually comes from this is: "I want people to be like me or to be impressed by me and I want to be known as a successful missionary." It's like when we pray the prayer of Jabez, not because we want God's territory to expand, but because we want our role in that expansion to grow. The aim should always be to make God famous. The aim should also be to ask the Lord not for fame, but for a great impact on His kingdom for His name's sake.

The significance of this movement—entering the mission— drives at the fact that when we are entering God's mission, it's not whether or not we may be tempted—because we will be. The question is: How do we deal with those temptations?

What I want to suggest is that we deal with those temptations by being more disciplined and more dependent. The longer we've been walking with Christ, the greater expectations we place on ourselves to be more mature. As I grow in the Lord, I have recognized that rather than me growing noticeably more and more mature—although that may be the case—what seems to stand out is how more and more ugly my sin is. What I thought wasn't that bad before is more and more pronounced. All the "big" sins may be gone, but the "little" ones are now just as gross and apparent. The other concept that seems more overwhelming is the fact that God is more holy than I could ever

have imagined. And in the same token, the more I walk with the
Lord and see my heart in light of the Word of God, I recognize
that I am more sinful than I ever knew.

In the beginning I thought obedience meant to stop cuss-
ing, backbiting, and gossip. Now I know obedience is not just
outward conformity, but inward obedience. This gap created a
separation with God—I am more sinful and He is more holy.
What I've seen in my life and in the lives of others, is that this
reality can lead to greater legalism or to greater dependence.
The legalist basically says, "You need to listen to me because I
don't struggle with what you struggle with." But that foundation is unstable when we recognize it usually leads many of us
to depression or frustration because we come to the conclusion
that our works are like filthy rags. They aren't good enough to
merit God's favor. On the other hand, this reality shouldn't lead
us to depression; it should lead us to greater dependence on the
Lord. As we fail and face our trials and temptations, we should
be led to dependence and not depression. That's why Scripture
calls us to grow in the knowledge of the grace of God (2 Pet.
3:18). That's why we continue to realize that what He did was
so much more than we could imagine in bringing us to Himself.

My oldest son is Dhati Lewis Jr. He is a great kid, an amazing athlete, and incredibly bright when it comes to academics.
His teachers love him, he is a friend to all, and he is just a peace-
able guy.

He struggles though—he aims for perfection, and the problem is, at times, *he seems to reach his goal.* So, when he is cor-
rected, we have to carefully guide him, because he can quickly
cling to sadness rather than dependence. We remind Dhati to
go above and beyond serving others proactively, because his
tendency is to forget.

We are to discipline ourselves as an admittance of our weakness. The missionary is to consistently spend time with the Lord,
consistently crucify the flesh, and consistently pray to remind
themselves that this is not about them but it's about God and

His power and His strength to accomplish both in and through us what He seeks to do in the world. The believer is to be reminded of these things through our spiritual disciplines. For instance, the purpose of giving is not to say that "I'm a good Christian because I tithe." We give 10 percent not because 10 percent is His, but to remind us that *it's all His.*

Giving the firstfruits reminds us of that truth.

CONCLUSION

As we enter God's mission, God allows trials and spiritual warfare to serve as diagnostic checks in our souls to question the authenticity of our calls and the integrity of our hearts. Welcome these and evaluate your heart carefully; welcome others to join you in this as you enter the mission. This will lead to being an authentic leader, one who can be trusted, one without the hidden agendas or the skeletons in the closet or the sketchy bank account.

I truly believe that authenticity is the apologetic of our day. People are not impressed with our ability to teach or preach or write. People watch and listen when they know you are real and authentic, and when they know you are being shaped and molded by the Maker. I see this in parenting very clearly. My children are not impressed that I can tell them what to do. They are not impressed because I teach them right and wrong. No, they are impressed when they see me growing up with them, when they see me clinging to the Lord for guidance and answers, and when they see me repentant for my harsh tone or my forgetfulness. This is true of the church.

You can teach what you know, but you only reproduce who you are.

You may be asking why this is important in our mission, and I would argue that it's important for a couple of reasons. The first reason authenticity is important is because people want to know if there is a God, and if you believe in that God, does He grip every aspect of your life? Or is He just something you do as an add-on to other things? I am consistently telling people that the world is not impressed when you get the same thing they get and you put a "Thank You, Jesus" at the end. They get a car and they say it was because of hard work; you get a car, and say it was God's grace—they are not impressed. People are looking for something real, something genuine; not an add-on to what naturally happens. They are looking for a faith that makes you reorient your life and shift your priorities, a faith that makes you stand with integrity and lead out in boldness.

Another reason it's important in mission is because trials and temptations often reveal our authentic selves. We must be honest with ourselves and be willing to assess our hearts so we can stay aligned with the Father. Self-assessment is a helpful "check-up" as we enter the mission and as we continue to engage in mission.

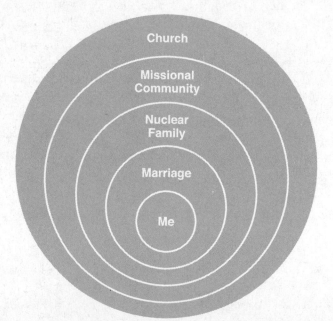

This is why, when I consider my five circles, I am intentionally asking the question on every one of those circles: Am I the type of person I want to see reproduced?

Do I have the type of marriage I want to see in my neighborhood?

Do I have the type of nuclear family I want to see?

Do we have the type of missional community we want to see reproduced?

Do we have the type of church we want to see reproduced?

And in each one of these rings, I put in intentional reminders, disciplines to cultivate the integrity and authenticity of *being* those things before trying to reproduce those realities.

CHAPTER 5

MOVEMENT #4 (PART 1): FRAMING DISCIPLE-MAKING

DISCIPLE-MAKING IS NOT *A* MINISTRY OF THE CHURCH; IT IS *THE* ministry of the church. Matthew 4:17–22 is the key text for the next movement. The passage reads:

> From that time Jesus began to preach, saying, "Repent, for the kingdom of heaven is at hand." While walking by the Sea of Galilee, he saw two brothers, Simon (who is called Peter) and Andrew his brother, casting a net into the sea, for they were fishermen. And he said to them, "Follow me, and I will make you fishers of men." Immediately they left their nets and followed him. And going on from there he saw two other brothers, James the son of Zebedee and John his brother, in the boat with Zebedee their father, mending their nets, and he called them. Immediately they left the boat and their father and followed him.

Matthew 4:17 starts out saying, "Repent, for the kingdom of heaven is at hand." Repentance is key here and involves many different factors. One element of repentance is a deep grief over sinfulness. If you are not grieved by your sin, you need to question whether or not you are a Christian because a Christian's life is marked by repentance. If you continue to boast and brag about your sin in the same way you always have, then your life is not marked by repentance. Once we change the way we see sin, we must secondly, renounce sin—turn from it. We no longer want to do things that grieve the heart of God.

Some would characterize this renouncing as sorrow, but it is more than remorse. When we renounce our sin, yes we are sad. But the sadness compels us to turn away from the sin and move closer to our holy God. Once we turn from our sin, we must, finally, forsake sin. Truly turning from our sin involves a sense of desperation. We cannot turn and forsake our sin unless we are desperate and dependent on the Lord. Why is turning and forsaking our sin crucial to Jesus' ministry? He answers this question in the second half of the sentence: because the kingdom of heaven is near.

Repentance also has another layer to it. The core of repentance means to change. Many times we only think about repentance in a negative way. We think of repentance when we have obvious sin in our lives and we need to turn from that sin. But really, the core of repentance is to change the way you see things. Jesus is introducing a new reality and vision for the kingdom of heaven and calling us to change the way we see it because the kingdom is at hand.

George Ladd, in *Theology of the New Testament,* defines *kingdom* as the dynamic reign or kingly rule of God based on a sphere in which the rule is experienced.[25] While there are many views on what the kingdom is, I will only elaborate on three. The first view promotes the belief that the kingdom of God is the church; and Jesus, who is head of the kingdom, rules over both the government and the church. The second view states that the kingdom of heaven is entirely futuristic; that we cannot, as the church, experience this kingdom that is to come. The third explains the kingdom of God as a both/and; "already, but not yet." There is a close resemblance between the church and the kingdom of God, but they are also utterly distinct. All three views can be found in different church traditions, and with differing points of merit, according to their points of emphasis. But it is important to clarify your definition of kingdom, because it is so central to the New Testament and Jesus' primary message while ministering on earth.

Notice that Matthew 4:17 does not say that the church is here. No, it says the kingdom of heaven is near. The church is a dim and poor reflection of the kingdom of heaven, which has yet to come fully. When the world sees the church, our desire is for them to say that while we are not a perfect people, we really love each other; we are a family. The church is God's way of showing the world what is yet to come—a family that loves one another perfectly. This is the hope of the gospel. In 1 Corinthians 13, Paul, the author, reveals that one day, faith and hope will not be needed because Christ will be with us again. But love will last forever!

When Jesus starts His ministry by proclaiming, "Repent, for the kingdom of heaven is at hand," yes, He was saying that we must see our sins differently because we offend a holy God. But repentance is about more than our justification; it is a core component of our ongoing sanctification. It is a central component of the church's ongoing march against the enemy. God wants the world to see this family, His church, taking sin seriously, loving one another, and changing the way they see the world based on the truths of Scripture. The picture we give the world will be a poor, dim reflection of the kingdom to come, but our love for one another stirs in us hope for the day when we will love one another perfectly.

Ongoing repentance is a core component of establishing a disciple-making culture. Without it, ego and pride can too easily corrupt the love of the community. But let's get even more practical. If establishing a disciple-making culture was the cornerstone of Jesus' ministry, how exactly do we accomplish that?

HOW TO DEFINE DISCIPLESHIP

To begin, let's start with a clear understanding of discipleship. I define *discipleship* as our *capacity to lovingly transmit and embody the life of Jesus through the life of His followers.*

I DEFINE DISCIPLESHIP AS OUR CAPACITY TO LOVINGLY TRANSMIT AND EMBODY THE LIFE OF JESUS THROUGH THE LIFE OF HIS FOLLOWERS.

OUR CAPACITY—THE ME AND WE

There are a few keywords in this definition I don't want you to miss. First, let's look at the phrase, *our capacity.*

There is a need to recognize that the conduit of disciple-making is the local church—the dim reflection of the kingdom of heaven. Whether you are a small group leader, missional community leader, ministry leader, or pastor—if you are mobilizing or gathering a group of people—you must rely on the local church in order to disciple! One must understand that it's both the *me* and the *we* for which we are responsible.

The first track to ponder is *your* life on mission—the *me*. We do this part well because of our American individualism. We can understand and begin to live out "my life on mission."

But the problem is that we too easily lose our corporate identity; the church's life on mission—the *we*. We tend to forget that God gave us our time, our talents, and our treasures in order to complete a missing link within the larger whole. It is our role to identify and recognize responsibilities of both our life and the church's life.

Any time you are mobilizing a group of people, you have to see it from both vantage points. Discipleship must be *our* capacity, not an individual effort. If, for instance, I was the only parent raising our children, we would have a bunch of bold, generous, and passionate kids without any discipline or structure to make it purposeful. It is when they are introduced to the *we* that they get Angie's discipline, order, kindness, and radical sacrifice. And, if Angie and I try to raise our children with only our individual capacities, they miss out on the others within the local body that can teach them trust, compassion, justice, and forgiveness. My underlying assumption when it comes to discipleship comes from an adaptation of an old African proverb:

> *My foundational belief is that if it takes a village to raise a child, it takes a church to raise a Christian.*

LOVINGLY

Another key word in the definition is *lovingly*. We are to lovingly embody the person and work of Jesus. We have to understand the means and the goal of discipleship. The Bible says the world will know you because of your love for one another (John 13:35). We transmit the gospel through love. In order to understand this, we need to understand the very foundation of sin. Sin is not simply breaking a moral code—it is a violation of LOVE. Sin is a violation of relationship. Jesus was asked, "Teacher, which is the great commandment in the Law?" And He said to him, "You shall love the Lord your God with all your heart and with all your soul and with all your mind. This is the great and first commandment. And a second is like it: You shall love your neighbor as yourself. On these two commandments depend all the Law and the Prophets" (Matt. 22:36–40).

Sin is anything that tears apart those relationships; it is not necessarily a defined act. For example, if I see my son hitting his brother, is that sin? Don't be too quick to assume that it is. It is all according to the heart and the context. Unfortunately, we tend to focus on behaviors and try to get kids away from certain behaviors, but that produces behavior modification instead of worldview transformation. In my example, the issue isn't necessarily hitting. If my son is choking on something, I want his brother to hit him on his back. The activity of hitting isn't sinful. If I am yelling at my kids, is that a sin? No. If they're about to get hit by a car, you want me to yell at them. In that situation, the most loving thing I can do is yell. The behavior is not the problem. We focus on the behaviors much more than the heart. God has said, "The world will know you are My disciples because of your love for one another" (John 13:35, author paraphrase). He is not looking for inauthentic outward obedience; instead, He is looking for an inwardly conformed, loving people.

TRANSMIT AND EMBODY THE PERSON AND WORK OF CHRIST

The next point of emphasis is that we are to embody the person and work of Christ. He is the substance. When we talk about the gospel, you can say gospel this, gospel that—gospel, gospel, gospel. But I find that people don't really understand what the gospel is.

Think about this. In a car, you've got Park, Reverse, and Drive labels on the gears. We know that when you put the car in D it goes forward and when you put it in R it goes backward, but the average citizen doesn't really know how the engine works. The same can be true about the gospel. When we talk about being gospel-centered, we don't really understand what that means. We understand what it means in justification (the one-time event when the Lord justifies your soul by purchasing your debt), but we don't know what Scripture means in sanctification (the process of growing to look more and more like Jesus). We get saved by grace. But we try to maintain it by the law. Paul addresses this very issue in Galatians when he writes,

O foolish Galatians! Who has bewitched you? It was before your eyes that Jesus Christ was publicly portrayed as crucified. Let me ask you only this: Did you receive the Spirit by works of the law or by hearing with faith? Are you so foolish? Having begun by the Spirit, are you now being perfected by the flesh? (Gal. 3:1–3)

We are trying to transmit the person and work of Christ to others. That's the goal of discipleship to be the embodiment of what Christ looks and acts like and, through the power of the Holy Spirit, transfer that into the lives of others. This task is daunting but we can find great comfort in that Scripture. Why? Because it has given us a clear picture of who Christ is. We no longer have to imagine what God looks like or who He is because like Colossians 1:19 states, the fullness of God dwells in Christ. All we have to do is look at Christ. When we look at Christ, we see the type of people God wants us to be. And when people look at us, they should see Christ embodied in our actions.

IMPARTATION INTO THE LIVES OF OTHERS

The last component of the definition is impartation into the lives of others. In Matthew 4:19, Jesus invited His disciples into relationship and then challenged them to change. "And he said to them, 'Follow me, and I will make you fishers of men.'" There is an invitation to walk with Him. There is an invitation to relationship. When you are called to come and follow, the assumption is you will be walking together, doing life together. The invitation is for relationship, but there's also a challenge to change. In following Christ, He says He will make us become fishers of men. In the Scripture, the disciples did not start as fishers of men, Jesus was making them into something new. When you are involved in disciple-making, you should assume you will be changed.

In his book *Building a Discipling Culture*, Mike Breen says, "No one accidentally creates disciples. Discipleship is an intentional pursuit."[26] No one accidentally does this. It's not something that comes by osmosis. There needs to be intentionality.

In Matthew 4:18–22 Jesus invites these brothers into a relationship with Him—into a family. Jesus called these men saying, "Follow me, and I will make you fishers of men" (v. 19). Jesus challenges these men to enter into relationship with Him and He challenges them to change. Too many times our churches will invite people to do one or the other—choosing between relationship and change. If we invite people only into relationship, we end up having a social club. If we only invite them to change, then we end up with a judgmental, critical group of people characterized by their condemnation of the actions and character of others. Developing a discipleship-making culture involves both relationship *and* change.

This blend of invitation and challenge is something that might be easier to think about in terms of a parent-child relationship. David Mathis writes,

> Beneath every manifestation of sin and rebellion in our children is some God-created good to affirm. Which means that pointed moments of discipline are not only opportunities to correct our children, but to connect with them. Our hardest times as parents are not just occasions to identify and punish the depravity in our children, but opportunities to identify and encourage their dignity. To parent their hearts, not only their behavior.[27]

A parent does not want their child to simply act the part and behave well without any heart involvement (no invitation/relationship) or to be completely spoiled without any behavior checks (no challenge). The goal here is balance. Mathis explains it as correction and connection.

It is the same idea that runs through this passage as Jesus invites these men into relationship (connection) while simultaneously challenging them to change (correction). These men knew what He was asking them to do—leave their occupations, their families, their livelihoods. Yet, their response was to follow Jesus swiftly and joyfully with great expectation.

Similarly, this is why membership at Blueprint Church is a call to discipleship. We are inviting people into a family called the church. And once you are a part of this family, you will be invited to change and look more like Jesus. We want you to be known by those in your family, which we accomplish through our missional communities. We want every member to be fully in—not two-thirds in, but all the way committed to relationship. When you commit to being in a missional community, you are committing to three things: gospel, family, and mission. You are committing to a group of people who will grow in the gospel, in the context of family, while living on mission. We invite individuals into relationship and challenge them to change—this is disciple-making in our church.

FOUR MAIN COMPONENTS OF DISCIPLESHIP

LIFE-ON-LIFE

Instead, I argue that there are four main components of biblical discipleship: life-on-life, theological training, leadership development, and mobilization.

There are four critical things for which every family of faith must wrestle. The first is life-on-life discipleship. Jesus said, "Follow me." At the very outset of His call, it was an invitation into relationship with Him.

If you were in relationship with me personally, you would not just see me in the capacity of mentorship—where I teach you something and ask you what you think. No. Instead, you would see me interacting with my daughters, you would see me handle an argument, you would see me bless the homeless, you would observe me handling my responsibilities, you would watch me in my weakness and strength. Many of us, however, have reduced discipleship to mentorship. Discipleship is not simply a one-on-one appointment twice a month with someone who is more mature in their faith.

When Angie and I were convicted early in our ministry about the importance of holistic discipleship instead of lopsided mentorship, we began to look for practical ways to change our ministry. This is when we first committed to tangibly using our home as a way to invite people into our lives. For most of our marriage, we have had people living in our home. And what we've learned is that it was an invitation into our lives. Instead of picking up the latest book and curriculum to study with others, we decided that our life would be our curriculum. In any community, individually and corporately, we must wrestle with the question: How are we cultivating life-on-life discipleship in our context? Inviting others to live with you is not the only way for life-on-life discipleship to occur. But for our church family, it has proved to be a vibrant and sustainable way to promote holistic discipleship.

It takes a whole church to raise a Christian. We cannot think of the church as an orphanage and create a culture of discipleship around that. Producing disciples takes a family. When someone asks you, "Are you your brother's keeper?" your response should be a resounding, "Yes!" Discipleship is a corporate endeavor; it cannot be done individually. You are absolutely responsible for the growth of your brother. There is no such thing as a healthy you if your church is unhealthy. That would be like saying I have cancer in my lungs, but my toes are as healthy as can be. Discipleship is not a meeting. It is not mentorship. It is not me teaching you what I know. It is not going through the latest Christian self-help book together. If this is discipleship, you will not find it in the Scriptures!

THEOLOGICAL TRAINING: GOSPEL FLUENCY

The second thing to wrestle with is theological training. How are we both lovingly embodying and transferring the person and work of Christ? When I talk about theological training, I'm not just talking about being better at Bible trivia. I'm talking about sitting at the feet of our Maker and understanding both who He is and what He's done for us. How are we cultivating a gospel-centered people where people are more fluent in the gospel, and their identity is more rooted in the person and work of Christ?

When we talk about this idea of being gospel fluent, it's the same as being fluent in any language. Take Spanish, for example. A lot of times people ask you, "¿Hablas español?" For people who understand a little Spanish, they often respond, "Hablo muy poquito." They are saying I understand the basics like "hello" and "how are you?" They can probably respond and say, "Fine, and you?" But if the person continues in Spanish, we may cut them off and say, "Oh no. *Muy* poquito." This is the same thing we often have with the gospel. We think about the gospel in a way that applies to the afterlife, but we don't have a gospel for the everyday. So we know what happens when we die; we just don't know what happens in the everyday. We don't have a gospel for today. We only know *very little* of the gospel. Theological training is teaching how to understand the person and work of Christ in light of our everyday. How can we become more fluent in the gospel and more rooted in our individual and corporate identity?

LEADERSHIP DEVELOPMENT

The third key to wrestle with is leadership development. How are we raising up and developing leaders in our church? Jesus says, "Follow me, and I will make you fishers of men" (Matt. 4:19). This comparison of giving someone fish to eat versus teaching that person *how* to fish is critical. In a lot of our discipleship relationships, we give people fish, but we never teach them how to fish. This produces a perpetual dependency on the person giving the fish. That's why we believe in worldview transformation instead of behavior modification. Behavior modification is me getting you to change your behavior because I said so. Worldview transformation is me helping to change your opinion about something and causing you to see it differently. For instance, I can tell you that you should never eat fried food (behavior modification) and you may listen to me and cut it out of your diet for a long time. However, if I teach you about what fried food does to your body and how the grease slowly clogs up your arteries, your view of fried food will shift and you will want less of it because you understand its effects. When we are training someone through a discipleship relationship, leadership development should be a huge facet.

Practically, how do we take a person from a new believer to someone who could be an elder? Our aim isn't for everyone to seek the position of an elder, but rather to strive for elder-like qualities because our ultimate goal is always to look more like our Shepherd. This should be our aim. What we have to do is think through the easy, obvious, and strategic steps for greater maturity and growth. In disciple-making, we do this by giving people age-specific responsibilities. All of my children have chores—they have had them since the age of two. When Dhati Jr. was three years old, we gave him the responsibility of setting the table. At dinnertime, we would put plates in his hands and walk with him to ensure he didn't drop and break a plate. One by one we would walk back and forth with him as he completed his job. It would have been easier and faster to set the table without him. But there was a greater goal than just getting the chore complete. We wanted to teach him responsibility. This is a family, not an orphanage—we needed him to grasp that. This is the same with discipleship within your church; we have to give age-specific responsibilities to help foster an understanding that all believers are to be responsible members of the family. For my son, over the course of time, we increased his responsibilities. As he grew older, taller, and stronger, he was able to handle more. (Now, at age nine, he cooks us breakfast!) In the same way, Jesus calls His disciples to become responsible family members. We don't need to just give fish away; we must teach others to become fishermen.

MOBILIZATION

Finally, the fourth component to think through is mobilization. Mission is a critical tool for sanctification. As we frame disciple-making, we need to get our people on mission. One of my first pastors, Tom Nelson, used to say, "Never teach a person the Bible without having them share their faith. If you teach without sharing, you'll produce arrogance. Because the only people who care about how much you know is other believers. But when you go out and share your faith, you realize ministry is not based on how much you know but you rely on a supernatural act of God to bring people to saving faith. This realization produces humility." If we want to be a part of making disciples who exemplify the humility of Christ, we must mobilize them to witness and reproduce the life-on-life discipleship they experience.

CONCLUSION

Making disciples is not optional for Christ followers. When Jesus left His followers on earth, He left them with a mission to carry on in His absence, and that mission was centered around disciple-making. Churches ought to be villages raising Christians. *Discipleship*, then, is our capacity to lovingly transmit and embody the life of Jesus through the life of His followers. It could also be said that it is our obedience to Christ's final command to His followers. Next, we will turn our attention to the Sermon on the Mount.

CHAPTER 6

MOVEMENT #4 (PART 2): THE IMPORTANCE OF THE SERMON ON THE MOUNT

GOD'S CALLING IS ONE OF ABUNDANT LIFE. THE CALL FOR anyone seeking to follow Jesus is to first deny himself, take up his cross, and then follow Jesus (Matt. 16:24). In reality, this call is not a call for you to lose anything; instead, it is a call for you to gain everything. The idolatry that runs rampant in our hearts can cause us to fall asleep to the things of God and the work He desires to do in and through us.

I'll never forget when I was in Honduras about ten years ago. We were there working with an indigenous people group and had made friends with the only other Americans in the town. I felt like we were really roughing it out there in the rain forest—no AC, sporadic electricity, limited running waters, and an outhouse with roaches and worms.

We had been to Honduras multiple times, so I had grown accustomed to the elements and had even gotten used to a different level of exposure to wildlife. During church services, bats would frequently fly above our heads. Moths were the size of my palm, large spiders frequented my room, and mosquitos were ten times the size of the ones in the States. But on this particular night, I was not prepared. We joined Roger and Katrina, our American friends, at their home by the water; Monopoly was on the agenda. As we were playing, I saw a rat scurry across the ceiling beam. I looked around, waiting for someone else to respond or react. But, it was like no one else saw the rat.

So I tried to tell myself to keep it cool, be tough like a missionary, and just push past it. A few minutes went by when I saw another rat. And then, a little while later, I saw a third rat. At this point, I hit my limit. I jumped up and said, "Does anyone else see this? There are rats in here!" The missionaries looked at me and began to laugh. I tried to explain to the missionaries that I am not used to seeing rats like this, but they continued laughing. I was so serious, but they couldn't stop laughing. And then, one of the women started laughing hysterically, and she just slumped over and passed out.

I was standing there like, "What in the world is going on here?!" She woke up for a minute, only to pass out again. They were used to the rats and thought my response was hilarious. Well, if this moment wasn't strange enough, it got better.

I looked at her husband and he just kept laughing. Fearful, I wondered if he realized his wife had just passed out. I was freaking out! It was in that moment her husband finally explained that I had just come face-to-face with a real example of narcolepsy. Before that experience, I used to think that narcolepsy was just a condition that made someone sleep too much; I had accused my best friend of having it many times. (I know, you're wondering what this has to do with the story, but just hang with me.) For those of you, like me, who may not know what real narcolepsy is, the formal definition is "a condition characterized by extreme tendency to fall asleep when in relaxing surroundings or during extreme emotions."

Okay, so back to the story. There were rats everywhere. This woman kept falling in and out of consciousness. And I felt like

I needed to get out of there quickly before something else crazy happened. So we finished the game and they walked us home. Although they thought our response was funny, they told us the next day that they noticed more rats than usual that night. After laying out traps, in the course of one night, they caught *thirty-three* rats—in their *house*. I was shocked and dumbfounded.

They referred back to that night countless times, and the more time spent with them, the more we saw Katrina's narcoleptic episodes. Sometimes it was from extreme relaxation, and other times it was because of extreme emotional conditions—anger toward her husband, happiness about a joke, frustration with the government for not getting the paperwork to approve a child's operation—I saw it many more times.

What's interesting is that many of us can go through our Christian lives with spiritual narcolepsy. In Matthew, Jesus is calling out to a group of spiritually narcoleptic people. They have been falling asleep. They became so accustomed to their spiritual condition (sin) that they relaxed and fell asleep. At the same time, others just as easily fell asleep when confronted with an intense conviction of an issue—they are numb to it. And when these individuals were asleep, they were not responding to the things of God—they were unable to do so.

The book of Malachi ends with a charge to God's people to repent and turn back to the Lord. The people of Malachi's time agreed to repent, but then they did not turn their hearts back to the Lord. Unfortunately, because of the lack of repentance, God's people experienced a silent era. For four hundred years, God went silent.

Four hundred years—that's multiple generations without a prophet to speak, multiple generations without men of God proclaiming His greatness, multiple generations where there was no vision for the people. We recognize that where there is no vision, the people perish—Scripture tells us that (see Prov. 29:18). And we see a great example of the fact that when relationship and communication with God ceases, religious legalism emerges.

Have you ever wondered how we got from the Old Testament worship of God as outlined in the law to the New Testament religious sects? These religious practices seemed to come out of nowhere! But it was during the time of silence that the people started to create their own laws[28]—"Where there is no prophetic vision the people cast off restraint" (Prov. 29:18). In Matthew, the Pharisees and Sadducees appear, and then the Maccabees and the Zealots. We see all these religious groups coming together and trying to work their way up to God. Their mind-set is, "If God isn't going to raise up a leader, we will do it ourselves." But God raises up John the Baptist to call the religious back to the Father. And can you guess what John's message is?

"Repent, for the kingdom of heaven is at hand" (Matt. 3:2, author emphasis).

THE SERMON ON THE MOUNT

God is calling His people to wake up out of their narcoleptic state, and He is calling them to repent because the kingdom of heaven is at hand. But in order for us to understand the call of Sermon on the Mount and properly apply it, we must first understand the context, then we must posture our hearts in humility, and then finally, we must identify our proper response.

As we aim to understand the context of the Sermon on the Mount, let's take a look back a few chapters before it happened. In Matthew 3, the author describes the baptism of Jesus. In Matthew 4, God leads Jesus into the wilderness, He is tempted three times, and He comes out of temptation through dependence upon God's Word and resistance to the lies of the devil. He then immediately initiates His ministry. From the very start, Jesus repeats the same message as John the Baptist—the message that God is calling us to renounce our former way of life and focus more on the inner issues of the heart in order to fall more in love with God and more in love with one another.

Picking up in Matthew 4:23, we read, "And he went throughout all Galilee, teaching in their synagogues and proclaiming the gospel of the kingdom and healing every disease and every affliction among the people." Here Jesus is giving a tangible expression of what the kingdom will be like in its fullest expression. There will be no death, no sickness, no tears, and we will all be healed. He is giving a firsthand experience of "already, but not yet." But, first, He wants His followers to understand that His kingdom is not about outward things; it's not just about changing the external things and practices in life—the healing, the comforts, etc. The number-one thing God is looking for is a changed heart. That's His aim. The problem is that too many of us, like the Pharisees and Sadducees, are too busy looking at the outward things and end up missing the whole point.

So Jesus continues preaching the kingdom and then we come to this part in Matthew 5: "Seeing the crowds, he went up on the mountain, and when he sat down, his disciples came to him" (v. 1). First of all, it's important to note that if Jesus was healing people in every town He entered, He was surely drawing a crowd. But it is critical for us to realize that the target audience of the Sermon on the Mount is not primarily the masses who showed up hoping for a miracle. The focus is on His disciples. The message is for God's people—those who He is calling out, those who have trusted in Him, those who are willing to take up their cross, deny themselves, and follow Him. As Jesus starts His teaching, He begins with the Beatitudes.

"Blessed are the poor in spirit, for theirs is the kingdom of heaven. Blessed are those who mourn, for they shall be comforted. Blessed are the meek, for they shall inherit the earth. Blessed are those who hunger and thirst for righteousness, for they shall be satisfied. Blessed are the merciful, for they shall receive mercy. Blessed are the pure in heart, for they shall see God. Blessed are the peacemakers, for they shall be called sons of God. Blessed are those who are persecuted for righteousness' sake, for theirs is the kingdom of heaven. Blessed are you when others revile you and persecute you and utter all kinds of evil against you falsely on my account. Rejoice and be glad, for your reward is great in heaven, for so they persecuted the prophets who were before you." (Matt. 5:3–12)

The point in this section is not to unpack each individual beatitude, but to look at the Beatitudes as a whole to understand the framework with which we should approach the Sermon on the Mount. Many scholars believe that you shouldn't look at the Sermon on the Mount until you come to grips with the Beatitudes. The reason for this is that within these Scriptures lies a heart posture that God is calling His people to live with.

First, the Sermon on the Mount calls God's people to identify with blessednesss. What does it mean to be blessed? To be blessed is to be happy. But this is not a circumstantial happiness. It is a happiness coming from the experience of God's divine favor. Jesus is making it very clear, the "secret" to happiness, to experiencing blessing, is not a secret. Those who have a heart posture that is poor in spirit, meek, merciful, and tender to the Lord, these are the people who experience the blessing and favor of God.

This emphasis on the position of our hearts is continued throughout the entire Sermon on the Mount. Later on Jesus says,

"You have heard that it was said to those of old, 'You shall not murder; and whoever murders will be liable to judgment.' But I say to you that everyone who is angry with his brother will be liable to judgment; whoever insults his brother will be liable to the council; and who-ever says, 'You fool!' will be liable to the hell of fire. . . . You have heard that it was said, 'You shall not commit adultery.' But I say to you that everyone who looks at a woman with lustful intent has already committed adul-tery with her in his heart." (Matt. 5:21–22, 27–28)

Jesus takes the laws we think we've mastered because we haven't murdered or committed adultery, and He attacks the heart of the issue. Just because you might be a little bit better at masking what's in your heart, doesn't mean you don't have an issue. The problem is not simply what you're doing. The problem is who you are—a sinner. That is what separates you from God. As we see this problem, our only response is a position and posture of poverty, to come before the Lord and say, "I am poor. I am bankrupt. There's no way in the world I can do or live up to any of this. All I can do is put myself in a posture where You can work in my life. Will You empower me through Your Spirit to live and do the very things that I'm called to do?"

Jesus is after our hearts, not our behavior.

Jesus ends the first and last beatitude with the statement, "Theirs is the kingdom of heaven." Recognize here that this blessing of receiving the kingdom does not come from what these people are *doing*, but from the posture of their hearts toward a God who has done everything on our behalf. This is why Paul writes in Philippians 3:8–9, "For his sake I have suffered the loss of all things and count them as rubbish, in order that I may gain Christ and be found in him, not having a righteousness of my own that comes from the law, but that which comes through faith in Christ, the righteousness from God that depends on faith." There is only one hero in all of the Sermon on the Mount, and it's not you and it's certainly not me. The only hero is Jesus Christ, God Himself. At the very beginning of this passage, by healing every sickness and disease (Matt. 4:23–24), Jesus is displaying the total authority that has been given to Him. And at the end, the response of the people is, "We have never seen someone with such authority" (Matt. 7:28–29, author paraphrase).

God is establishing a new kingdom and is bidding us to come and join Him. But the kingdom is not about you or me; it's about Him. He calls us to come and posture our hearts toward Him. He calls us to recognize and identify with blessedness. He calls us to understand what it means to establish a kingdom built on a posture of repentance; He changes our view of Himself. We should see Him higher and more lifted up than ever before as we give Him the authority that's due His name.

The Sermon on the Mount is where we see the charge for followers of Jesus to initiate the new kingdom experience through radical inward change. This type of transformation becomes a reflection of the fullness of the kingdom that is to come, providing the world with an opportunity to experience the kingdom of God in its "already, but not yet" state. All the while, we are to hold high the work of Christ and look toward the day when He will transform our imperfect reflection into a glorious reality.

CHAPTER 7

MOVEMENT #5 (PART 1): A CALL TO DISCIPLE-MAKING— A CALL TO LABOR

MY WIFE CALLED A FAMILY MEETING ONE NIGHT. SHE HAD started a new job working at the local elementary school and was coming to the realization that our family did a great job letting her serve us. She presented her case to us: "There are many things that need to happen throughout the week for everyone's days to go smoothly. We need breakfast and lunches for school and work, which means we need someone to go to the grocery store. We need clean clothes for school and work, which means that someone will need to do laundry on a regular basis. We need dinners each night, which means that someone needs to cook. We need rides to basketball practice and soccer games, so someone needs to drive. (You could see the wheels turning in the kids' heads—we need a cook, a maid, a chauffeur, and a chef . . .) And, you need a sane mother, so that means that someone needs to sign up to do all these things!" She continued as she pulled out a chore chart and then had everyone sign up as laborers for each of the tasks.

Jesus' strategy of disciple-making seems counterintuitive and could even be deemed as unsuccessful if we measured it by our modern-day standards. Jesus' strategy was to call the lowly, the common people, and to invite anyone who would follow. Our culture tells us that in order to be successful, you first gather all the stars and shiny people to follow, then others will see the popular people following and they, in turn, will follow as well. Not Jesus. He had a motley crew following Him, and to this crew, He dedicated nearly all of His time.

In fact, those whom He would spend most of His time on earth with were a family of uneducated, untrained, regular, blue-collar men. We need to repent for our mule-mentality that demands we shoulder the burden alone. Jesus' model was to empower His followers to *do* ministry together.

THE HARVEST IS PLENTIFUL, BUT THE LABORERS ARE FEW

Jesus dedicated most of His time to the twelve disciples. If you study the lives of these disciples, you will find they were all very common men—so common that in Acts 4:13 the Pharisees (the religious leaders, educated people, saints, the ones who went to seminary) labeled the disciples as "uneducated, common men." However, they also noted that the men "had been with Jesus."

We can gain so much from looking at how Jesus was a disciple-maker. Although the idea may be foreign to us, the truth is that being *sent out* to labor is not based upon our qualifications, it is based upon the qualification of our Savior. I am confident that Matthew wanted to make sure we understood this. In this chapter, we will explore what it means to be sent by answering the following three questions:

1. Why does Jesus call His disciples to labor? (He could certainly do it all on His own!)

2. How does Jesus call His disciples to labor?
3. Why are the disciples called to look to Christ as they are laboring?

WHY WE LABOR

Matthew reveals why we labor, how we labor, and why we look to Christ as we labor.

And Jesus went throughout all the cities and villages, teaching in their synagogues and proclaiming the gospel of the kingdom and healing every disease and every affliction. When he saw the crowds, he had compassion for them, because they were harassed and helpless, like sheep without a shepherd. Then he said to his disciples, "The harvest is plentiful, but the laborers are few; therefore pray earnestly to the Lord of the harvest to send out laborers into his harvest." (Matt. 9:35–38)

Through the first nine chapters of the book of Matthew, Jesus has only asked the disciples to watch. Watch Him heal the sick and give sight to the blind. Watch as He prays, watch as He engages with the outcast, and watch as He teaches the Scriptures. But now Jesus is making a shift. He is aiming to help the disciples understand that the kingdom of heaven is near. How do we know this?

In Matthew 8–9, we see Jesus perform ten miracles—Jesus cleanses a leper, heals a paralyzed servant, heals Peter's mother-in-law, calms a storm, heals two men who were demon-possessed, heals a paralytic, raises to life the daughter who appeared to be dead, heals a woman who had a issue with blood for twelve years, heals two blind men, and gives the mute the ability to speak. Jesus does all these things in just two chapters!

Why is Jesus doing all of these miracles? John and Matthew make the answer clear: *so that we may know that Jesus is the Son of God.*

The miracles validate that Jesus is the Christ. If we were to survey the Bible, we would discover only three periods when miracles were performed at this level. First, Moses performs great miracles—first before Pharaoh, then before Israel. Then God performs miracles through Elijah and Elisha and other prophets. Now we see Jesus and eventually the apostles performing miracle after miracle, all pointing people to understand that God is sovereign and is with those performing the miracles. The kingdom of heaven is near, so near that it is with them in human flesh.

At the end of chapter 9, Jesus is traveling from city to city and all the villages, teaching in the synagogues, proclaiming the gospel, and healing every disease and every affliction, and something amazing is happening: thousands of people follow Him. As He heals the sick and gives sight to the blind, people are in awe of what they see. We need to stop here and recognize one thing: Jesus is blatantly challenging our ideas of successful ministry.

Everywhere Jesus is going, thousands of people are being attracted to Him, many people are being healed, and miracles are performed. Everywhere Jesus is going, He is speaking to many people and attracting thousands and thousands of people. Today, any of us called into ministry would want this to happen; thousands of people following us sounds like a great accomplishment, a blessing. But, Jesus' response was different. He looked out over all the people and the Scriptures read, "He had compassion for them" (Matt. 9:36).

This appears to be successful, but what's interesting is how Jesus responds to what's going on. In verse 36, Jesus has a totally different response than the one you and I would most likely have. Instead of being excited and overjoyed at the massive audience, Jesus was overcome with a depth of compassion that made Him physically ill. The word *compassion* carries the connotation that Jesus was sick to His stomach; His bowels were wrenched. Jesus was bent over, frustrated because the people were leaderless; they didn't have someone to lead them.[29]

And the question is: In the midst of this thriving ministry, in the midst of going from city to city and healing all of these people, what would bring Him to this physically ill, gut-wrenching compassion? Matthew gives us the answer: "because [the crowds] were harassed and helpless, like sheep without a shepherd" (9:36). Jesus explains to His disciples that He is not content to draw a huge crowd and perform miracles. All of the people coming are helpless and harassed and *they are still shepherdless*. They don't have anyone walking with them in an intimate way. This is *why* Jesus calls us to labor: His people need leaders to follow!

HOW JESUS CALLS

Jesus makes it clear that He is not excited about dropping into a city, doing a lot of good deeds and miracles, and then bouncing over to the next city. None of our personal methods, models, principles, or practices could ever create a better ministry than Jesus had. And yet, how often are we content to go somewhere, put on a big event or give an extravagant gift, and then head back to our lives of comfort? Jesus felt physically ill when He experienced the same scenario.

We have turned Christianity into conferences, concerts, and church services. We have defined Christianity as mission trips, activities, or simply the events that we do for God. But Jesus' response to our massive gatherings would be the same as it was to His own massive gatherings—He was grieved because the deepest needs of the people still went unmet. Even though He is healing their sickness and diseases, those who were following Jesus still have a huge problem—they are without a shepherd. There is no one to walk alongside them.

When Jesus looks at the crowd, He does not see success in numbers. He responds with the utmost compassion because after His miracles are complete, they still will not have a shepherd to lead them.

In response to this, Jesus calls His disciples to labor. In Matthew 9:37–38, Jesus says, "The harvest is plentiful, but the laborers are few; therefore pray earnestly to the Lord of the harvest to send out laborers into his harvest." There is a shift happening in these verses.

For the first time, Jesus is moving the disciples from watching Him do ministry to actually exhorting them to labor.

The wonderful part about Jesus during this shift from having the disciples *watch* to having the disciples *do*, is that He tells them how to do it. He gives four definitive actions to explain how He is calling us to labor. Jesus calls the disciples:

1. to see with clarity,
2. to feel with compassion,
3. to pray with confidence, and
4. to respond with closeness.

See with Clarity. First, Jesus says the disciples need to see the crowds the way He sees them. The crowd is just a crowd like any other crowd. There is nothing wrong with them. They are plentiful; their number is without end. The problem is not with the crowd. The problem is with the laborers. There are not enough people to shepherd those in the crowds. The religious leaders God left in charge of the crowds are too busy critiquing Jesus and criticizing His efforts. So if they are not going to lead God's people, who will?

This passage in Matthew 9 is similar to the passage in Ezekiel 34, and the Israelites should have recalled Ezekiel's words: "My sheep have become a prey, and my sheep have become food for all the wild beasts, since there was no shepherd, and because my shepherds have not searched for my sheep, but the shepherds have fed themselves, and have not fed my sheep" (Ezek. 34:8).

God put people in place to shepherd His people, but instead, they turned it into something self-centered. The same thing that they were rebuked for in Ezekiel shows up again in Matthew as Jesus is, once again, addressing the issue of shepherdless sheep.

God knew this day would come when those He put in charge of His children would abandon their call and make ministry about themselves. But He tells Ezekiel that He will respond by personally coming to shepherd His people! We must see this with clarity: The problem is not the harvest; the problem is not that there aren't enough people who want to listen to the gospel. The problem is that there are not enough shepherds and not enough leaders.

Harvest, as you may know, is a farming term. Farmers spend much of the year tilling, fertilizing, and planting seeds with the hope that all their work would produce a crop or "a harvest." They wait and wait, praying for just the right amount of rain and sunlight and no harsh frost; they pray that the harvest time will be plentiful. The time for harvesting is very significant—there is only a certain time frame farmers have to gather the crops. If they take too long, the produce will rot, resulting in an economic loss. The owner of the field cannot harvest the crop fast enough alone. So, during the harvest time, everyone is called to labor. They have one opportunity to retrieve the crop in a timely fashion and it takes a lot of hands to accomplish this very important task. Jesus is explaining to His disciples that the harvest of the kingdom is plentiful. It's abundant and large and ready to be harvested! But the problem is, there are not enough laborers to work the field.

Feel with Compassion. Jesus not only calls the disciples to see with clarity, He calls them to feel with compassion. We must see crowds of people with clarity. A large crowd does not represent successful ministry. A large crowd does not indicate successful pastoral shepherding. We need to look at large crowds with the same compassion of Christ because they do not have a leader to lead them. Who is going to answer the questions they face on

Monday? Who is going to walk beside them through grief and doubt? Crowds become an indicator of success only when we have made our ministries self-centered.

Jesus did not view the gathering of the masses as an indicator of effective ministry.

He was grieved because He knew they had no one to shepherd them.

Responding with compassion always drives us to dependence on the Lord because we cannot meet the needs of the masses on our own. As we become more dependent on the Lord, we are compelled to pray. So, as we labor with clear vision and feel deep compassion, we are led to pray with confidence.

Pray with Confidence. Jesus says, "Pray earnestly to the Lord of the harvest to send out laborers" (Matt. 9:38).

Pray. Prayer is the very first thing Jesus calls His disciples to *do*. This whole time they have been watching Jesus do ministry. But now, their first call to action is prayer.

Prayer is not a call to passivity. It is an activity that calls for purpose and determination. We are communicating with the God of the universe, ultimately saying we are utterly and completely dependent on Him. In our relationship with God, all we bring is need and we need Him to respond with compassion. We can have confidence when we pray because we are asking the sovereign God to move on our behalf. He can do all that we are unable to do and more. When Jesus calls us to pray, He says for us to pray earnestly. We sense a desperation in the word *earnest*. We are to pray as if everything is on the line; pray like we have everything to lose unless God intervenes.

In addition, this phrase "send out" is only mentioned twice in the New Testament. It comes from the Greek word *ekballo*, which means "to force out." He is telling us to pray with desperation that the Lord would force us out of our comfort to serve the masses of people wanting to follow Jesus.

If we were honest, we would admit there are many aspects of our lives that trump our call to go out and serve the masses of people wanting to follow Jesus. We are so consumed with our own families, jobs, needs, bills, sicknesses, and trials, that serving others is placed low on our priority list.

To pray to be forced out does not feel safe and is often frightening. We do not naturally choose to pray or act in this way. It's very similar to the way a mother eagle teaches her chicks to fly. Eagles wait until their eaglets are about two months old and, when it's time, they take their eaglets in their mouth and fly with them up to the highest point. Then, they drop them—they force them out. At this point, the baby eagle has two choices: fly or die. The eaglets would never leave the comforts of the nest if the mother eagle did not force them to fly. The same is true for us. God knows we will always follow the path of least resistance because we like comfort, we may even be addicted to it. We won't naturally become laborers and leaders if God does not force us out, causing us to do so.

Jesus essentially tells His disciples, "Pray to the Lord of the harvest. Pray earnestly, but as you pray, pray that God would force us out, force us out of our comfort." We see a prime example of this taking place in Acts 6. It starts in a similar fashion, with a very successful ministry. Conservative scholars say there were probably thirty thousand people who were saved within the first year of the church. Other scholars believe up to fifty thousand people were saved. We look at these numbers and think, "How much more success could you have?!"

People are being saved, right? People are coming into the church. But the problem is that in Acts 1:8, Jesus says, "You will be my witnesses in Jerusalem and in all Judea and Samaria, and to the end of the earth." Jesus' followers were content with looking at their ministry success and saying, "We're good. Look at what God is doing. He obviously doesn't want us to leave this. We are here, and all of these people are coming to know the Lord. We need to stay together. We're just getting a chance to know one another. We have the same culture. We have the same context. Our ministry will be stronger if we stick together."

There's just one problem. God said go.

Go to Jerusalem, Judea, and the outermost parts of the world. His design was not to have them stay together in comfort. So what does God do?

He forces them out using the zealous church persecution from Saul of Tarsus. In the midst of Acts 7, Stephen, the faithful preacher of the gospel, was stoned. In the midst of this, we are inclined to ask, where is the grace of God? We see the answer in Acts 8 where Scripture reveals that because of death, because of persecution, because the church began to be ravaged, because of Saul, the word of God began to spread in Judea and Samaria— He sent them out.

But even as He pleads with us to pray, He gives us even more clarity about how to pray. We are not to simply say, "Lord, save the people in my town. Lord, just please save the people in my neighborhood." And then we get up, lay the burden aside, and go eat dinner. That's not the type of prayer for which Jesus is asking. Jesus is asking for earnest prayers that align with His will as we say, "Lord, we want to see the gospel established in our neighborhood. And we want it desperately. Force us out even if You have to bring disease, even if You have to bring persecution, even if You have to bring—whatever You have to bring, let Your will be done on earth as it is in heaven. Don't leave it up to us because, see, the reality is that, Lord, I might be convicted by the message right now, but I know by Sunday night, other things in my life are going to crowd out the very thing that I was desiring to do. So, Lord, don't allow it to depend on me. Please, force me out."

Have you ever prayed a prayer like that?

If left up to us, we would always reconceptualize Christianity and warp it with our own drive for comfort. We will gather in churches and conferences and concerts. We will continue to cluster in our little Bible studies while the rest of the world lives as helpless sheep without a shepherd. If we don't step up, leave our comfort, and lead others, our churches we love so much will fail.

Matthew is illustrating in these chapters that God is the God of the harvest; no one is beyond His reach. As we go before our Father, we pray to Him, understanding that He is not just Lord of our church services. He is also Lord of our neighborhood. He is Lord of our city. He is Lord of the people we are afraid of, and He is Lord of the people nobody else wants. We pray with confidence that God is able and will force us out of our comfort despite ourselves. He says, "Pray to that Lord, the Lord of the harvest," and it is in that where we find that we can pray with confidence because there is no harvest outside the Lordship of our God.

Like Jesus, we should not grow comfortable doing one-time events; generosity here and a salvation story there. These are good deeds, but Jesus wants more. Yes, He wants us to see people the way He sees them—with clarity. He wants us to feel compassion when we see the crowd because they are helpless and harassed, like sheep without a shepherd. And we are to pray with confidence that the Lord will force us out of our comfort in order to lead others.

Respond with Closeness. But finally, we are to respond to the needs of the crowd with closeness. A shepherd is primarily known for being *with* the sheep. Jesus wants us to model our ministry after His own. We should spend time with those whom God puts in our midst, we should challenge and teach them. It is through presence with people that we see them move from being converts to kingdom builders!

The exciting part of this passage is Jesus eventually reveals that His prayer for more laborers is answered—"pray therefore to the Lord of the harvest to send out laborers . . ." (Matt. 9:38). The prayer is answered! Guess who the answer is? The disciples. You. Me. Our churches. The answer is not our pastors and those who "really" study the Bible, but it's all those willing to forsake all to labor and lead God's people.

What's interesting about this passage, however, is the fact that Jesus is calling His disciples to do the very thing that He was doing. Although His ministry methods may not have been successful from a worldly perspective, His ministry is what produced the believers that are alive today. The church is not an orphanage; it is a family. We cannot afford to run church like an orphanage. The laborers cannot be just a few people while the large majority enjoy the comforts those few provide. Every one of us needs to carry our weight and take responsibility because the harvest is plentiful; the laborers are few!

My prayer is that each of you would begin with a foundational understanding of your call as a sent-one, that you would respond by seeing, feeling, praying, and responding with closeness, and that every one of you will personalize this call. Jesus' call to labor is not a call to the masses. This is a call to you because the harvest is plentiful, but the laborers are few. I pray that by the Holy Spirit, God would force us out to do the very things we desire to do, but simultaneously stray away from doing. And I pray for you, that the Father would strengthen, protect, and encourage you with His closeness as you embark on this journey.

CHAPTER 8

MOVEMENT #5 (PART 2): AMONG WOLVES

REMEMBER MY CONVERSATION WITH THE DIRECTOR OF THE Boys & Girls Club about fatherlessness? When I first moved to Atlanta, I took a visit to a neighborhood called Lakewood Heights. I was trying to learn the city and it was suggested that we start with the Boys & Girls Club, so I went and began speaking with the director. I asked a few questions, not knowing that what I learned would shape the rest of my life. I asked, "How many children do you serve on a consistent basis?" The answer: two to three hundred kids weekly. The next question and answer floored me.

"How many of these two to three hundred kids have both mom and dad in the home?" He looked at me and said, "What's that?" He was joking, then seriously responded and said, "I can count on two hands those who have both mom and dad in the home."

I was grieved and cried out, "Lord, why doesn't it seem like You are calling anybody to *this*?" Lakewood Heights is a poor, crime-infested area. My wife and I drove down several of the streets, stopping to talk to the neighbors. My wife asked one elderly woman how she liked the neighborhood. She responded and shared that her home had been broken into several times that month, but other than that, she liked it.

This was a neighborhood where men in the home were nonexistent—there were no dads. My heart sunk. This neighborhood doesn't need more volunteers. It needs men, invested men who fear God. It needs dads, husbands, and leaders.

The problem at the Boys & Girls Club will not be solved by drop-in volunteers. The solution is not a healing ministry; the solution is not more acts of service. The problem is they are shepherdless. The only solution is for shepherds! This is an area that needed to hear the faithful words of our Savior, "I will never leave you. I will never forsake you. I am here with you." There was no one in this neighborhood saying that very thing—"I will never leave you, your problems are my problems." That type of commitment is a tall order—especially in hostile environments.

"Behold, I am sending you out as sheep in the midst of wolves, so be wise as serpents and innocent as doves." (Matt. 10:16)

To be as wise as serpents is to have a good capacity to understand circumstances: it is to be cunning. Basically, Jesus is telling the sheep to have a little street sense.

One of the misconceptions about sheep is that they are totally dumb animals. But Christ wants to make it clear, He isn't sending dumb disciples. He is making sure the disciples understand they are not to walk among wolves with stupidity. Instead, they are to be wise as serpents. While it is true that sheep may not be the brightest animals, they are well-known for their strong following instinct. When a sheep goes into a hostile environment, they are actually quite intelligent. They understand they have no real protection, except their strong flock instinct. A sheep gets anxious whenever they don't see other sheep around. As soon as a wolf comes, the natural instinct for sheep is to come together.

The thought is we are more protected together than we are alone as strays. They have this instinctual response to gather together.

BE WISE, BE INNOCENT

Many of us look at Christianity as a pursuit for protection. But it is not a pursuit of protection; it is a fight against isolation. Sin isolates us. To be wise is to understand, whenever I'm in trouble I need to look for the other sheep in order to find protection.

Jesus goes on and adds that we are also to be innocent as doves. To be innocent as doves literally means to be "unmixed." It refers to the purity of our intention. Basically, don't be a hustler.

So on one side He says have some street sense. And on the flip side, don't have unmixed desires and focus. He calls us to keep our motives pure so we don't ever give anyone a reason to feel like we have selfish ambitions or manipulative motives.

John Piper says, "When Jesus says that he is sending us as sheep in the midst of wolves, he means that we will be treated the way wolves treat sheep."[30] That doesn't really give us any comfort, does it? Jesus is saying in Matthew 10:16 that the call to be sheep among wolves is ultimately a call with the certainty of vulnerability in the midst of persecution. Jesus is saying, if you are really with Him, there is a guarantee you will face persecution. Not a maybe, not a small chance—it is a very certain reality.

As I wrestled with this text, I began to ask the question, "Can sheep even survive by themselves in the wild? Even more, can they survive among wolves? Why in the world would Jesus send His disciples on such a dangerous mission?" Naturally, my initial response was to conclude that this verse cannot mean what it looks like. Initially, we might be tempted to think Jesus didn't mean what He said. This is why Dr. John Ewart, from Southeastern Baptist Theological Seminary, says that 95 percent of evangelical Christians never even intend on sharing their faith,

never intend on making any type of disciples, and never intend
to obey this verse. We have turned the Great Commission into a
mild suggestion. It is easy for us to read something like this and
quote it at appropriate times, but when it's time to actually go
live it out, we argue that it doesn't make any sense to be vulnerable in this way.

Our flight from vulnerability has created a lack of real power
or presence anywhere outside of our protected Christian environments. It is in these environments we've instituted an active
teacher with a bunch of passive listeners—we have a pastor and
the congregation, or the Bible study leader and those in atten-
dance. We have reduced Christianity to one active teacher and
many passive listeners. And what do we do as we try to duplicate
"Christianity"? We go to our jobs and start to rally up the other
Christians and duplicate the pattern: I'll be the teacher and you
sit here and listen and now I'll create a bunch of passive listeners.
We have, in the end, tamed the gospel and reduced Christianity
to concerts, conferences, and church services—minimizing the
way we experience God. We have no clue what God looks like,
feels like, or even how He would have us move among wolves
because we are so comfortable with our protected environments.

Look at the verse again in Matthew 10. Jesus says He is
sending us *as sheep*. The problem is not that we are sheep. The
problem is not that sheep are vulnerable. The problem is that we
are people without *shepherds*.

What is a shepherd primarily known for? Being *with* the
sheep. The Bible shows us two kinds of shepherds: a lowercase-*s*
shepherd and a capital-*S* Shepherd. The lowercase-*s* shepherd is a
call for us to identify with the sheep as shepherds—the harvest
is plentiful and the laborers (shepherds) are few. He's reminding
us that it's not just about us going into a neighborhood, giving
a bunch of turkeys, and then going back out and feeling good
about ourselves. It's not about doing "drive-by ministry" where
you drive in, drop off something, and leave. No, the need is for
shepherds who will be committed to being present. Shepherds

who will live among and be *with* the sheep. In this passage, the lowercase-*s* shepherd is not a call to a position (or a pastor) but a call for the practice of presence.

Don't forget the context. Jesus has been doing some amazing things. In Matthew 8–9, it's as if God turned the dimmer light switch up high and it is blazing. We see God through Jesus Christ coming and performing miracle after miracle after miracle. Jesus is on tour, going from city to city, village to village, and the people are sensing God's presence. Obviously, this comes with intense joy and excitement.

Look at Matthew 9:33, the crowd responds by marveling and saying, "Never was anything like this seen in Israel." What Jesus did was not normative. Matthew is telling us to stop and recognize that never in the history of all of Israel has anyone ever seen someone like Jesus.

And now, Jesus commissions His disciples, and His disciples are now called to do the very thing that Jesus was doing—they are called to be the shepherds. You can imagine the disciples in that moment, feeling like everything was too good to be true. Everything was going so well. Jesus was healing and performing amazing miraculous feats. So it probably seemed abrupt when Jesus began ordaining and commissioning them to do the same. After all, they are only sheep.

In Matthew 10:16 Jesus captures the attention of His disciples and says, "Behold." The word "behold" means to gaze upon, to perceive with our visual faculties. Jesus is calling for a use of the imagination.

He says, "Imagine, in the midst of all these great things going on, imagine being persecuted because of Who you believe in. Imagine that I still want you to bear witness of Me in the midst of that persecution. Imagine that you need to persevere faithfully to the end."

In the midst of everything going so well, Jesus asks the disciples to stop and imagine their worst nightmare coming true. He is not trying to hide the cost of following Him. Becoming shepherds would come with significant cost. Shepherding is a dangerous calling.

Jesus made it clear from the very beginning that following Him will be costly, but for some reason we often forget that. At the beginning of our walk with God we are so excited about all the new things we are promised. We are promised abundant life, deep-rooted peace, and secure joy. But it seems as soon as we follow Jesus, all of a sudden we become the prime target of the Enemy, and life gets more complicated than before. The cost seems greater.

Jesus comes down hard right here in the midst of all the prosperity and celebration and says, "Listen, there's a reality you need to understand and come to grips with. Even though you're following Me, you don't have a king's X on you. There will be persecution." The truth of the matter is, if you are on mission, persecution will happen. In the face of that reality, Jesus gives us three things to consider.

He calls us to:

1. prepare for persecution,
2. proclaim Christ in the midst of persecution, and
3. persevere in light of persecution.

This was the call to be laborers, to be shepherds.

PREPARE FOR PERSECUTION

Matthew 10:17–25 reads:

[17]"Beware of men, for they will deliver you over to courts and flog you in their synagogues, [18]and you will be dragged before governors and kings for my sake, to bear witness before them and the Gentiles. [19]When they deliver you over, do not be anxious how you are to speak or what you are to say, for what you are to say will be given to you in that hour. [20]For it is not you who

speak, but the Spirit of your Father speaking through you. [21]Brother will deliver brother over to death, and the father his child, and children will rise against parents and have them put to death, [22]and you will be hated by all for my name's sake. But the one who endures to the end will be saved. [23]When they persecute you in one town, flee to the next, for truly, I say to you, you will not have gone through all the towns of Israel before the Son of Man comes. [24]A disciple is not above his teacher, nor a servant above his master.[25]It is enough for the disciple to be like his teacher, and the servant like his master. If they have called the master of the house Beelzebul, how much more will they malign those of his household."

Jesus tells His disciples different ways we will be persecuted if we are on mission. The first you see in verses 17–18 where He explains that we will be brought before authorities. For many American believers, persecution by authorities is most likely to come through work and interaction with our bosses. For most, sharing the gospel at work is not "allowed," but oftentimes that is when we have opportunity to share, because those are the relationships we have built. In sharing, someone could be offended and they can complain to the boss and the boss could reprimand or terminate used based on proselytizing. This is persecution. Other believers will experience more intense persecution by police, courts, and government offices. Regardless of the intensity, the truth is—persecution *will* come.

Jesus goes on to say that not only will you be brought before authorities, you will also be betrayed by family.

My wife's family had a very difficult time with her following the Lord and marrying me. It caused division and rejection—to this day she does not have a relationship with her sister.

A brother in our church came to know the Lord. He came from a Muslim background. In accepting Jesus, this brother was saying good-bye to his family because he knew for certain that they would reject him and his new faith.

Jesus says you can count on this happening to you. Brothers will go against brothers. Children will rise up. Your family will tear apart.

PROCLAIM CHRIST IN THE MIDST OF PERSECUTION

Jesus continues and says *you will be hated by all people.*

Jesus uses imperatives to be as clear as possible. It is as if He is saying, "I am sending you out in the midst of wolves and while being in the midst of wolves you will be vulnerable. There will be authorities to persecute you. There will be family members who won't understand and will turn away from you. There will be a general consensus that the world doesn't like you. They think that *you* are their problem."

If you are reading this and you haven't experienced this type of persecution, just go and preach the gospel explicitly to your friends and family. I'm not talking about living lovingly before them; I'm talking about *preaching* the gospel. Jesus says that when you proclaim that He is the only way, you will be persecuted. Preach the gospel and see how tolerant your friends and family are with you.

As if that wasn't enough, Jesus says we will be persecuted and ultimately run out of town. You will be slandered and defamed. Imagine, if they called the master Beelzebul, how much more will they defame you?

Imagine being called a homophobe.

Imagine being called a sexist.

Imagine being called a bigot.

Imagine being called whatever they call us—not because they're making up stuff, but because you're simply preaching God's Word, because you're saying Jesus is the only way, the only truth, the only life, and anyone who doesn't believe is going to hell. You didn't make that up. You're just quoting the Bible. But you're a bigot because of it.

I'm not talking about finding persecution for persecution's sake. I'm talking about if you just stay in the text and reiterate God's Word in love, the world will slander you, they will hate you, you will lose friends, and you will be brought before governors for your stance—you will be persecuted.

For us as Americans, we don't often have to deal with the more intense ramifications of that reality. Researchers vary in conclusion, but the International Society for Human Rights estimates that at least seven to eight thousand Christians are killed for their faith each year.[31] In America, this is not the case. Instead, our greatest fear a lot of times is being embarrassed, the fear that others may not like us. Jesus is sending us out among wolves, and whether it be losing friends or losing our lives, He is letting us know the cost up front.

Prepare for the persecution as you go out as shepherds.

PERSEVERE IN LIGHT OF PERSECUTION

I love Charles Spurgeon's quote in relation to this passage. He said, "A sheep in the midst of wolves is safe compared to a Christian in the midst of ungodly men."[32] Jesus tells the believer that we need to prepare because not only are there possibilities of persecution, but if on mission, it is a certainty.

But when persecution happens, don't worry. You are in the center of Jesus' will. Does that statement surprise you? It doesn't sit well with most of us because so many of us define God's will by the path of least resistance, as if God is always calling us to easier and better. We are addicted to our comfort and we think God's number-one priority is to preserve us. But Jesus says, "No. I am *sending* you among the wolves and you *will* face hardships and persecution."

You might ask, if sharing my faith brings so much trouble, why in the world would I even start sharing my faith? It doesn't make sense. Why would we do that?

Jesus would answer simply, "Whoever wants to be my disciple must deny themselves and take up their cross and follow me" (Matt. 16:24 NIV). But this is why Jesus commands us to pray that God would force us out because, left to ourselves, we would not go out and witness in these conditions. We must pray that God would put us in a position where we have to share. That we would be deeply uncomfortable with anything less than whole-hearted obedience. But not only that, Jesus sends us for a particular purpose and a particular reason. And we have to come to the recognition that every Christian has been sent to be both bold and blameless in the midst of persecution. It is not an elective for some who choose to be brave. It is a commission. It is an imperative. It is a commandment. And Jesus is not blind to the realities of what will happen if you obey.

Don't allow the persecution to hinder you. Why? Because we've always been persecuted. Jesus says His prophets have always been persecuted. Why? Because they hate Him. Don't take offense. They hate Jesus. He is the dividing line.

Even in the midst of all the miracles, healing everyone, and doing nothing but showing compassion, at the end of Matthew 9 there is a group accusing Him of doing work based on the power of Satan. Don't take persecution so personally. They hate us because they hate Jesus. Yet, Jesus reminds us that He is orchestrating all of this so we may proclaim Him in the midst of it and then He challenges us to persevere to the end of it.

Charles Spurgeon says it this way, "He who has gone on to prepare heaven for us will not leave us without provision for the journey."[33] So you ask, what is God's provision for perseverance in persecution? The answer is simple: His presence. His presence is our provision. If you walk through the book of Matthew, you see it's all about presence. He never promises us escape from persecution; He only promises to be present with us.

The problem is, as John Piper states, many times we believe the lie that God delivered us from the wrath of man. God's deliverance, however, was to save us from the wrath of God, not man. In the midst of persecution, what's the worst thing man's wrath can do to you? If death is the worst they can do, you will get to be with Jesus. Physical death is not worth fearing. Jesus calls us to remain faithful and persevere with confidence in the promise of His presence. In Matthew 9:36 the sheep were helpless because they were without shepherds. But in Matthew 10:16 He says, "I am the shepherd and I am sending you."

Look back over this pattern of presence in the book of Matthew. In Matthew 3, God is with Jesus supernaturally in His baptism and says, "This is my beloved Son, with whom I am well pleased" (v. 17). In Matthew 4:17–23, the call is to follow Jesus, to be with Him. Then later on, He calls us to go into the harvest and labor *among* the harvest, to be *with* the harvest. Later on He says He is building His church and we see the idea of the need for God's people to come together and be present with one another. And then, look ahead to how Matthew ends. The greatest commission of all: "Go therefore and make disciples of all nations, baptizing them in the name of the Father and of the Son and of the Holy Spirit, teaching them to observe all that I have commanded you" (28:19–20), and how does it end? Presence. Jesus says, "And behold, I am with you always, to the end of the age" (v. 20). God promises us His presence. His presence is His provision.

His presence encourages us to view persecution differently, but it also empowers us to endure. He tells us not to be anxious when they deliver us because He will give us the words to speak when it's time. He says, "For it is not you who speak, but the Spirit of your Father" (Matt. 10:20). I really believe that right here we are supposed to understand the familial nature of His encouragement. He could have said the Holy Spirit, the power, or any other variation of the word. But how does He identify? He says "the Spirit of your Father." He is tenderly encouraging us to remember that in the midst of it all, even though your brothers, your friends, and the world will reject you, He is your Father and He will send you the words to say.

This is the story of the Christian life. This is the story of walking with God. You see it all throughout Scripture. You see it with Daniel, with the Hebrew boys, over and over again they are brought before judges, men, and authorities who tell them to deny God. The devil tempts Jesus to deny God in exchange for all the pleasures and power the world can offer.

We have to look back and come to the same conclusion God's people have come to time and time again.

Yes, you can put us in this furnace or in this lions' den. And this lion could eat me. And this furnace might burn us up. But guess what? It is better to be with our Father than to bow down to a false god.

To be with God is more precious and valuable than any safety, security, power, or pleasure the world has to offer. Why do we do such ignorant things according to the world's eye?

Because we have been sent.

Because we are His.

Paul came to this gripping reality in Acts 19 when there was a riot in Ephesus because of his work. After the riot and continued persecution, Paul gathers the elders of Ephesus and tells them,

> And now, behold, I know that none of you among whom I have gone about proclaiming the kingdom will see my face again. Therefore I testify to you this day that I am innocent of the blood of all, for I did not shrink from declaring to you the whole counsel of God. Pay careful attention to yourselves and to all the flock, in which the Holy Spirit has made you overseers, to care for the church of God, which he obtained with his own blood. I know that after my departure fierce wolves will come in among you, not sparing the flock; and from among

your own selves will arise men speaking twisted things, to draw away the disciples after them. Therefore be alert, remembering that for three years I did not cease night or day to admonish every one with tears. (Acts 20:25–31)

My prayer is that we would begin to take on the heart of God, the heart of Paul. That we would not define God's will by the path of least resistance. That we would not allow our sin to keep us in isolation from Him or His people. I pray that we would not deny His call but we would count the cost and do exactly what He has called us to do.

The question is not, what do you want to do with your life? The question is, what is Jesus doing and how do we join Him where He is moving in the world?

We are following a person. This is not theory. This is not just something to conjure up in our own minds.

"So have no fear of them, for nothing is covered that will not be revealed, or hidden that will not be known. What I tell you in the dark, say in the light, and what you hear whispered, proclaim on the housetops. And do not fear those who kill the body but cannot kill the soul. Rather fear him who can destroy both soul and body in hell. Are not two sparrows sold for a penny? And not one of them will fall to the ground apart from your Father. But even the hairs of your head are all numbered. Fear not, therefore; you are of more value than many sparrows." (Matt. 10:26–31)

Jesus says, "Here is the plan. I'm going back to Jerusalem, and when I go back I'm going to die." And the very thing we're thinking, Peter is bold enough to blurt out. He says, "Jesus, that's a dumb idea." And Jesus responds and says, "Get behind Me, Satan" (see Matt. 16:23).

Why? Because Peter is thinking like man. He thinks the ultimate goal is self-preservation. This is not about self-preservation.

This is about doing the will of the Father. And not only that—if any of you want to follow Jesus, you must also take up your cross, deny yourself, and follow Him (Matt. 6:24). Jesus was letting us know that if you follow Him, He is about the will of the Father and this is also our call as disciples.

DO NOT FEAR

Jesus is not ignorant of the reality of our hearts and our minds and what that stirs up inside us when we hear that type of language and persecution. It brings about fear. We are afraid of so many things. And Jesus is not blind to that.

I really believe that some tensions in our lives are not meant to be solved, they are meant to be managed. So how do we manage our fears in the face of persecution?

Most of us have probably been taught to avoid fear. Don't be afraid of this, don't let fear control you in that. . . . Can you hear your parents telling you to not be afraid?

I was that dad and, sadly, I still am that dad sometimes. When I ask my son to go get something from the dark basement, he may say, "Dad, can you come with me?" My response is, "Boy, if you don't get down there and overcome those fears . . ." Have you been there? We've been taught not to have fear at all. Jesus recognizes it though and understands that we have fear and it is actually a good thing—it's something that comes with being human.

Ultimately, fear is not evil. It is simply an emotion that tells us we are not in control. Fear can lead us to try and take control of things—I'm afraid of people, or spiders, or whatever it is and we try to control our environment because of the fear. This response is what leads 95 percent of Christians to determine not to share their faith—the thought being if I don't, then I can control persecution from happening to me. However, the other option is that we can allow fear to lead us to greater confidence, faith, and wisdom in the Lord.

N. T. Wright says, "'Fear not' is the most frequently repeated command in the entire Bible."[34] Managing our fears is important because a mismanagement of our fear can silence our witness. It will keep us from wisdom. Chip Dodd says, "Fear offers the opportunity to trust God and others with our need for help **or** it entices us to stay stuck in the distrust and self will."[35] The Bible tells us that the beginning of wisdom is a fear of the Lord (Prov. 9:10). A mismanagement of our fear can cripple us from experiencing God's presence. But a well-placed fear can lead us to wisdom, rooted faith, and greater intimacy with the Father.[36]

If you know the story, in Numbers, Moses sends twelve spies to check out the Promised Land. They return with a report that the land is exactly as God said. It is flowing with milk and honey, beautiful, and flourishing. But there is a problem. It's also filled with a bunch of giants. Ten out of the twelve spies who went in, came out and said, "We will not go back because we will surely die." Only two said, "We will go because God is with us and surely He will conquer all that needs to be conquered."

However, the Israelites follow the ten spies and refused to enter into the Promised Land because of fear of the giants. Because of their disobedience, the people then had to wander in the wilderness for forty years. Anyone over the age of twenty-one was never allowed to experience the promises found in the land. Finally when it was time to go into the land and leadership had been transferred to Joshua, God begins with Joshua in the same way He did with Moses. He says, "The same way I was with Moses. I am with you. Fear not, be strong and courageous. Be strong and courageous" (Josh. 1:5–7). Four times in Joshua 1, Joshua is reminded to be strong and courageous. Why? Because God is *with* Joshua.

God didn't change the reality of the land. God didn't kill off the giants or the kings of Canaan. He didn't do any of that. He didn't change the outside world to make it more palatable. That wasn't His objective. He was waiting until His *people* were more palatable, until His people were willing to trust Him more than their fear. And guess what? In the midst of going into the land, there were some people who lost their lives. If you're in war, there will be casualties. But you also see in the book of Joshua, the Lord's army was 21–1, with the only loss coming because of the sin of Achan in Joshua 7. God's presence overcomes fear. But many times, our mismanagement of our fears will keep us from experiencing God's presence.

CONCLUSION

In closing, I want to make three quick points that Jesus recognized in the midst of persecution.

First in Matthew 10:26–27, God's promises encourage us to face our fear of persecution. It says this, "So have no fear of them, for nothing is covered that will not be revealed, or hidden that will not be known. What I tell you in the dark, say in the light, and what you hear whispered, proclaim on the housetops." Right here He is reiterating that the way we are to properly manage our fears *is* by trusting in God's promises. God's promises encourage us to face our fear in the midst of persecution.

What do I mean? He is telling us, don't have fear of them because everything that is covered will be revealed. We have a special privilege today to have such great access to the Scriptures that were written for us. We have Genesis *and* Revelation. We get a chance to see a *complete* picture of what's going on and what will come at the end. It may look like we are losing right now, but the ultimate outcome is victory.

We are to be on mission for Him. At times it may feel like we are losing the battle. But we get a chance to realize that He will reveal all things and that all things will be given to us. It's like knowing the score at the end of the game before you watch it.

You watch the game, and your team is down by twenty points. Yet, you know the final score and it gives you the ability to watch with a confident hope that the tables will soon turn. Jesus is saying to us, "Don't be afraid because I promise you, at the end, this thing all works for the good of those who love the Lord." He has shown us the score at the end of the game. Even in the midst of tragedy, we have the ability to have confidence.

The second point is that God's power gives us proper perspective with which to place our fear. Verse 28 says, "And do not fear those who kill the body but cannot kill the soul. Rather fear him who can destroy both soul and body in hell." Essentially, Jesus is saying, "Listen, the worst they can do is kill you. You'll be physically dead but spiritually alive with Me. That's the worst they can do, so don't fear them. Instead, put your fear in the One who can kill both soul and body." Jesus is flexing His muscles! He's showing His sovereignty.

Imagine walking down the street and being confronted by a mini-Chihuahua barking at you. Even if you're not afraid of dogs, you might be a little startled, a tiny bit frightened. But you continue to walk. Then, you see a pit bull charging at you; all of a sudden that little Chihuahua is like a distant reality compared with this greater fear. Jesus is not downplaying our fears as much as He is challenging us to put our fear in its proper place. Our fear needs a reality check because God is the One who is all-powerful and sovereign. Fear of man pales in comparison to the fear He deserves. We are to fear the One who is greater. God's power should give us proper perspective for our fears.

The most beautiful part of all of this—and this is the third point—is that God's protection allows us to trust Him in the midst of our fears. I love verses 29–31 where He says, "Are not two sparrows sold for a penny? And not one of them will fall to the ground apart from your Father. But even the hairs of your head are all numbered. Fear not, therefore; you are of more value than many sparrows." Right here it's as if God says, "Listen, the ultimate reality is that we are going to win. The ultimate reality is that I am all-powerful and they are not."

Even in that, some of us wrestle with feeling like we are invisible. Our team might win, but what about me? Am I just a casualty in the midst of all of this?

Jesus stops and says, "Listen. You, yes you, are valuable. You are a significant part of this. The reality is that even the sparrows, who are worth a couple of pennies, not even those will fall to the ground apart from Me allowing it to happen. I know how many hairs are on your head. To the very smallest of details, I value you. I'm concerned for you. In the midst of all this persecution, I got you. I will never leave you. I will never forsake you."

As He is sending us out, He is constantly reminding us to trust Him—not if He changes the external realities, but to trust him *in* our realities.

I really believe many of us are not experiencing the abundant life that Jesus has called us to and I think it's because of this gripping fear that prevents us from serving and being on mission with our God and King. We are functioning as two-thirds Christian.

We are good with the gospel and have a decent understanding of Scripture. We are good with community and enjoy being part of a family. But we have no real explicit and intentional relationship with those who are outside in the world. Because of a lack of those relationships, we aren't experiencing God's grace in a way we can only experience when we are on mission with Him, joining Him as He rescues lost souls.

BRINGING IT ALL TOGETHER

Here are a few application points to bring all of this together. First, we have to be mindful and disciplined to remember that God is alive and active. Do you have constant reminders placed in your life? How are you cultivating discipline to remember that He is alive? That's why it's important to come to church and hear the testimonies of His people so that even though you may not feel like God is active, you can hear the testimonies of God's people and you can hear how God is moving and, in turn, be reminded that He is not an absentee landlord. Be intentional to build in disciplines to cultivate constant reminders in your heart to build trust that God is alive and working.

Second, we need to be vulnerable to God, ourselves, and others. We fear vulnerability. But it's in vulnerability we have the ability to say, "I am afraid, but I choose to be willing to show that Christ is greater than my fears." He doesn't tell us to lose our fear; He tells us to manage our fear. Instead of placing our fear in the things we can't control, He is telling us to place our fear in the One who can control.

And the question is: *How can we embrace God in the midst of our fears?*

The last challenge is to be all in. Don't be afraid of failure. Many of us seem to hold out a little because we are afraid to be all in. We want to reserve a little bit because we are afraid to fail. Even if we fail in this life, we can know that we won't fail in the one to come. We know that God wins because He has revealed all things to us and He tells us to trust in His promises and power in all things.

His presence is the fuel that empowers us to be all in, without hesitation, living fully as those sent to be sheep in the midst of wolves.

CHAPTER 9

MOVEMENT #6: TRAINING FROM SERVICE

NOW IT CAME TO PASS THAT A GROUP EXISTED WHO CALLED themselves fishermen.

During those days, the streams and lakes were teeming with fish, and the fish were constantly feeding. Complex ecosystems of fish abounded, and waterways were bursting at the seams. The lakes, rivers, and streams needed to be fished. All that the world needed at that time was this new group: those who called themselves fishermen.

Week after week, month after month, and year after year the fishermen met and talked about their call to fish, the abundance of fish, and how they might strategize together to better fish. They built power plants to pump water for fish and tractors to plow new waterways. Others felt their job was to relate to the fish in a neighborly way, so the fish would know the difference between good and bad fishermen, while others felt that simply telling the fish that they were nice, kind, land-loving neighbors was enough.

In all the meetings, the fishermen would carefully define fishing, defend fishing as an occupation, and declare that fishing is always to be the primary goal of fishermen. These fishermen built large, beautiful buildings called fisheries. At every meeting of the fishermen, the plea was always the same—everyone should be a fisherman and every fisherman should fish.

There was only one problem—*no one actually fished.*

Until one day, a young fellow left one of the meetings and actually went fishing. The next day he reported that he caught two outstanding fish. He was honored for his excellent catch and was whisked off to share his story of how he caught a fish. He was a hero.

Eventually, attending the meetings and conferences took up all this young man's time, so he quit fishing in order to tell how he caught two fish. He was placed on the fishermen's general board and hailed as someone having considerable experience in the fishing business. Though he still, obviously, called himself a fisherman, he no longer had any margin in his life to actually bait a hook, launch a boat, or cast a line.

Imagine how hurt some were when, one day, someone suggested that those who do not fish were not fishermen, no matter how much they claimed to be.

Is a person a fisherman if year after year he never goes fishing?

Is one following the plea to fish if he never throws his line into the water?[37]

I am sure by now you get where I am going with this. This story is intended to be both convicting and funny, and I believe it reflects the state of the church, especially in America.

We talk a lot about making disciples—being fishers of men—but very few of us actually *go* fishing for men.

In previous chapters we talked about movements in Matthew where Jesus develops the DNA of disciple-making. First we discussed the importance of seeing the church in the context of community. The church is not doing well simply if an individual is doing well. The church flourishes and grows when everyone takes responsibility for one another and everyone is flourishing and doing well. Second, we discussed the importance of seeing the church as a family, not an orphanage. Too many times, a few people will labor hard, but will inevitably leave the church members undernourished, all while the few laborers become overworked and burned out.

Next, we discussed the importance of establishing a disciple-making culture in the church by laboring together. Unlike the story I opened this chapter with, we are to serve one another and be active fishers of men, not just talk about laboring and fishing. We prayed that the Lord would force us out of our comfort and make us labor in His harvest as sheep and shepherds among wolves. From here, I am going to move on and spend the rest of this chapter defending Jesus' exhortation to labor for the harvest.

WHY BOTHER?

I remember when I first became a Christian, I was so excited. I wanted to absorb all I could about the Bible and Christ and growing in my newfound faith. When I would hang out with my Christian friends, I soon discovered that the Christian faith was about a lot of things I can't do. I can't go to the club, can't drink, can't join a fraternity, and can't have sex before marriage. All of these things are good to abstain from, but what was I sup-posed to do? What exactly was Christ calling me *to* do? Instead of being solely reactionary, how could I be more proactive in my faith?

After spending time studying the Bible and learning more about my faith, I soon discovered that Jesus was calling me to co-labor with Him. For the first time in my Christian life, I knew what I was supposed to do—make disciples and be a fisher of men. This new concept was revolutionary.

The question still looms: *Why bother?* What is right for you is right for you and what is right for me is what is right for me, right?

I have mentioned it before, but one of the saddest, most disturbing stats I have ever read is that 95 percent of evangelical believers never intend to share their faith.[38] Talking about fishing and planning for fishing and praying about fishing are so much easier and less threatening than actually fishing. But Jesus says the harvest is great, but the laborers are few. The laborers are few. What might He mean by the latter part of this statement and what might be His remedy?

Through Jesus' example, we see a clear answer—focus on a few faithful men! Making disciples is a spiritual discipline. It does not occur through osmosis or philosophy; it occurs when we are actively pursuing it. So many Christians confess to living a mediocre life in Christ—nothing close to the abundant life described in John 10:10. I believe the biggest reason for apathy is we are guilty of omission of mission.

Let's look at the story in Matthew 14:13–21:

> Now when Jesus heard this, he withdrew from there in a boat to a desolate place by himself. But when the crowds heard it, they followed him on foot from the towns. When he went ashore he saw a great crowd, and he had compassion on them and healed their sick. Now when it was evening, the disciples came to him and said, "This is a desolate place, and the day is now over; send the crowds away to go into the villages and buy food for themselves." But Jesus said, "They need not go away; you give them something to eat." They said to him, "We have only five loaves here and two fish." He said, "Bring them here to me." Then he ordered the crowds to sit down on the grass, and taking the five loaves and the two fish, he looked up to heaven and said a blessing. Then he broke the loaves and gave them to the disciples,

and the disciples gave them to the crowds. And they all ate and were satisfied. And they took up twelve baskets full of the broken pieces left over. And those who ate were about five thousand men, besides women and children.

FIVE REASONS WE SHOULD LABOR FOR THE HARVEST

1. *Laboring for the harvest grows us from passivity to compassion.* In Matthew 14:13 it says, "When Jesus heard this . . ." What did Jesus hear? Apparently there was an event that took place that caused Jesus to withdraw in a boat to a desolate place. Matthew 14:1–12 reveals that the event was the death of His cousin, John the Baptist. John played a tremendous role in the launch of Jesus' ministry on earth. He prepared the way for Jesus to baptize with His Spirit by baptizing with water. John the Baptist proclaimed, "Repent, for the kingdom of heaven is near" and Jesus proclaimed the exact same message.

If John had died by natural causes, I am not sure Jesus would have responded the way He did. But John's death was the result of foolishness. King Herod was at a dinner party where there was wine and food and dancing. Herod became drunk and decided to impress all of his friends. He called his daughter in and told her she could have anything she wanted. So she went to her mother, Herodias, and told her what her father said. Without any hesitation, Herodias said she wanted John the Baptist's head! Once Herod heard his daughter's request, he was deeply grieved because he liked John, but his wife hated him (John called out Herod for having a relationship with his brother's wife). Not wanting to lose the respect of his peers, Herod had John beheaded and his head brought to his wife.

Mark 6:31 reveals yet one more reason Jesus and His disciples pull away to a desolate place—they are tired. Jesus and the disciples had been on a mission trip, laboring all day and night. Jesus and His disciples were headed in a boat to the other side of the lake to get some rest and time away from the crowd. To their great surprise, a crowd awaited them.

Can you imagine working all day with so many people who have lots of physical and spiritual needs and are looking to you alone for answers? (Even if you are a pastor, you can't relate to the depth nor breadth of the ministry burden Jesus shouldered.) Imagine, after a sixteen-hour day you head home looking forward to your La-Z-Boy and a glass of iced tea. Once home, not only are there more needy people in your front yard waiting for you to help them, but there is someone sitting in your favorite chair and drinking your favorite tea! Unlike the disciples, Jesus didn't get frustrated and angry that they needed help. He was moved with compassion "because they were like sheep without a shepherd" (Mark 6:34). Jesus was not passive in His response, but moved *toward* the crowd. John Onwuchekwa, a good friend and fellow pastor in Atlanta, defines passivity as an act "when a love for self crowds out the ability to love others."

Many times we camouflage passivity as being spiritually or emotionally mature. People tell me all the time to slow down and take time for myself. Their thought is that if I don't slow down I might burn out. I agree there is a time to rest, but if we are relying on the strength of Christ to enable us to do the work He has set out for us to do (Eph. 2:10), we won't burn out because He is our strength. Another way we camouflage passivity with maturity is not having difficult conversations when we need to have them all in the name of salvaging relationships. This is not maturity, just classic passivity. What we are saying when we do this is, "I love myself and how I feel more than I love the other person and our healthy relationship."

Jesus does not respond passively even though He would have been justified in doing so. He responds with compassion. Jesus is addressing idolatry of self, an issue which is running rampant in America. Some would say America's biggest idols are money, power, or control, but *I believe our biggest idol is love of self.*

Jesus is modeling loving others as a discipline and a key part of disciple-making. Spending time in quiet with the Lord is good, but the source of our quiet time is more critical.

Many Christians only give generously when they have excess—more time, more money, more things. Jesus models what it looks like to give out of lack—fatigue, exhaustion, and weakness. Another example of giving out of our lack is found in John 4 when Jesus tells His disciples after a long day of work that they must travel through Samaria. He sends them off to get food while He has a life-altering conversation with a woman at the well. Once the disciples return, they tell Jesus He has to go because He is tired. Jesus' response? "I have food to eat that you do not know about" (John 4:32). Something else fuels Jesus.

2. *Laboring for the harvest aligns our heart with His, taking us from "rational" to "irrational".* What the disciples tell Jesus is not unreasonable. The day has been long and draining, and Jesus is grieving John the Baptist's death. To insist that the people go buy and acquire their own food and start back in the morning makes sense. But, not to Jesus. Jesus does not agree with their "rational" thinking.

Jesus said, "They don't need to go away. You give them something to eat." And they said, "Well, we only have five loaves here and two fish." He said, "Bring them to Me." Jesus is radical in everything He does. His decision to feed the masses at the end of a long day seems extreme.

Making disciples and being fishers of men does not always make logical senses. Paul sums up this radical truth when he says, "For, if we are beside ourselves, it is for God; if we are in our right mind, it is for you. For the love of Christ controls [compels] us" (2 Cor. 5:13–14).

Paul gives us even more compelling evidence in Philippians 2:5–8 to live more radical, irrational lives for the sake of the gospel:

In your relationships with one another, have the same
mindset as Christ Jesus: Who, being in very nature
God, did not consider equality with God something to
be used to his own advantage; rather, he made himself
nothing by taking the very nature of a servant, being
made in human likeness. And being found in appearance
as a man, he humbled himself by becoming obedient to
death—even death on a cross! (NIV)

Why did Jesus sacrifice so much for us? Why did He bother
to do this? Jesus sacrificed everything for us because He "did
not come [to earth] to be served, but to serve" (Matt. 20:28).
He is establishing a new way of thinking, especially for leaders.
Leaders serve; they do not wait around expecting others to serve
them.

**3. *Laboring for the harvest establishes our identity, remind-
ing us that we are God's chosen vessels.*** When Jesus tells His disciples not to send the crowd of needy people away, but they are
to serve them, the emphasis is on "you" doing.

We have all heard the phrase, "If you don't praise the Lord,
the rocks will cry out." This statement was made by Jesus when
the disciples were praising Him, and the Pharisees asked Jesus to
silence their praise. Jesus tells them if we keep quiet, the stones
will cry out (Luke 19:40). Jesus does not want rocks praising
Him; He wants us, the ones He has chosen and died for, to serve
Him and praise Him. Paul reminds us that it is not us who have
the strength and will to make disciples, but God who is making
the appeal through us.

I will never forget what God did in my heart when I visited the Boys & Girls Club and witnessed firsthand all of the
fatherlessness in the cities. Everyone wants and hopes that cities
around the world will look and be better, but we are waiting on
someone else, even God, to make the sacrifices necessary to see
the change happen. Jesus is compelling us in His actions to let
down our nets—to be willing to leave our livelihood and take

up our cross—to be willing to sacrifice everything for the sake of the gospel and follow Him wherever He leads. We are God's vessel of change. Jesus tells the disciples and us today to go and feed the crowd even in our fatigue, and rely on the Lord to make the appeal *through* you.

4. *Laboring for the harvest reminds us of our inadequacy and compels us to pray.* When the disciples ask Jesus if they are to go buy the food, they seem anxious. The Gospel of Mark brings clarity. In order to feed the crowd, they could need to spend thirty days' worth of income. Can you imagine thinking Jesus was asking all twelve disciples to spend an entire month's salary on feeding this crowd?

We are so much like the disciples. When God is summoning us to follow Him, we come up with all kinds of excuses why we cannot do what He is asking. Moses said he stuttered, David said he was too young, Sarah said she was too old, Mary said she was not married yet, and we say we have not been to seminary or don't have enough money or we are now married with children. But Jesus tells us all that we are His vessel of choice and we have His strength and resources to complete the job.

We tend to only put ourselves in positions to do the things we already know we can do on our own, but God is calling us to so much more. We must recognize that ministry is supernatural. What we are trying to do is beyond our capability. If your ministry can be contained or controlled or explained logically or rationally, then you are probably not doing ministry the way that God has called us to do it.

What is Jesus calling us to do? Envision going to the cemetery and speaking to a tomb saying, "Rise from the dead!" This is what Jesus is calling all Christians to do when He says for us to be disciple-makers and fishers of men, except we are speaking to zombies, not tombs. We are compelling people who are physically living, but are dead spiritually, to come to life. Only God can do this supernatural work; we cannot. All we can do is be God's vessel and rely on His strength and power to bring life where there is death.

Ministry is humbling work. Last Thanksgiving our missional community prepared food and brought plates to a local hotel to give to those who might need food to eat. I remember praying, asking the Lord to do something—bring people to Himself, save them. Guess what? None of my prayers were answered that day. We spent a lot of time and resources to offer this small token of love to people we did not know and no one placed their faith in Christ. Not only that, but they were going to be hungry again in just a few hours. So why do we labor when it seems futile?

5. *Laboring for the harvest reminds us of this sufficiency strengthening our faith.* God wants *us* to do this work—countering our flesh—driving us to pray because on our own we cannot make a lasting difference in people's lives.

Sometimes making disciples and fishing for men is like spitting in the air. We spit and spit and when the wind blows, it hits us in the face. People laugh at us and say why do they continue doing this? Are they not embarrassed by now? Yes, serving the Lord by serving His people can be embarrassing and humbling, but it compels us to pray that the Lord will change the direction of the wind. We cannot do this, only God can. We depend on Him to shift the wind. While we labor in service and prayer, Jesus wants us to feed the crowd. We are tempted to complain about what we do not have, but God will always tell us to bring to Him what we do have. He will take our lack, bless it, and multiply its impact.

In Matthew 14:13–21, the emphasis was not on the large crowd. The Scriptures say there were five thousand present, but most scholars believe the actual number was somewhere between ten and fifteen thousand (including women and children). The crowd had no idea Jesus did not have anything to feed them. They probably were not expecting them to feed them. The focus of the passage is on the disciples witnessing a miracle, being trained for mission as they serve alongside their leader.

CONCLUSION

The crowd will get hungry again in three to four hours, so saving the crowd from hunger cannot be the overarching point, and it is not. The big aha moment is for the disciples; their lives are forever changed because they got to witness God take what little they had and multiply it in a way that only God could do. When God sends us out, we are constantly dependent on the One sending us out. And when we witness a miracle, there is no greater feeling in the world.

We must stop praying selfish prayers that only focus on what we need and start praying prayers for others to be saved. When God answers those prayers—the supernatural ones—our faith grows in leaps and bounds.

Does the leadership of Blueprint Church believe we will plant churches in Decatur and the West End and Smyrna and Ellenwood? Yes, we do. But we also pray that each member of Blueprint will be in awe of what God does through little ol' us. We are God's chosen vessel to make disciples and fish for men. He wants to change us and grow us, while meeting the needs of others.

Yes, this passage is about the disciples and what happened in them. Not only was the crowd satisfied, but there were twelve baskets left over for the disciples to be reminded of the miracle Jesus pulled off. They started with lack and ended with abundance. This story in Matthew reminds me of the story of the widow, her child, and the prophet Elijah. Elijah approaches a widow who is down to her last food supply. She was preparing for her and her son to die after their last meal when Elijah asked her not to fix the meal for them, but to fix it for him! And this is what she did and the results were more than she could have imagined. She had enough oil and flour to last her a lifetime. We can experience this kind of life in Christ, but we have to get beyond ourselves.

Missions doesn't just happen by accident; we must discipline ourselves in all areas so we can pray for the Lord to grant us opportunities to serve His people. Christ was fatigued and tired, but He was moved with compassion and He expects the same response from us.

If you are experiencing the abundant life Jesus promises to give us, you are probably witnessing the following: 1) growing in your understanding of the gospel; 2) connecting with a group of people who are your family; 3) living on mission where you are. The problem is many of us think we can experience the first two, while neglecting the third one and still live an abundant life. This is another example of passivity—the love of self crowding out the ability to love others. Yes, God can make the rocks praise Him and give witness to who He is, but He wants to use *us* as His vessel.

The gospel changes people, and people change the world.

CHAPTER 10

MOVEMENT #7: MOBILIZING CORPORATELY FOR MISSION

A. W. TOZER SAID, "WHAT COMES INTO OUR MINDS WHEN WE think about God is the most important thing about us."[39] In a similar vein, I'd like to suggest that what comes into our minds when we think about church is the most important thing about our ministry. I have learned through church planting that everyone approaches church with notions of what the church is (or should be).

For some, church is the place to experience the comfort of community. For others, church is a place to go to for uplifting inspiration. For many, church is where they turn for moral guidance and support. For some, church is how they keep their nuclear family together and intact. Still, for others, the church is a defender for truth where their particular favorite doctrines are espoused and explained. While there is truth in each of these notions, they do not tell the whole story, nor are they the picture of the church as Jesus envisioned it.

Promoting a correct picture of the church is important because people will give their time, talent, and treasure toward a vision. If we want people to lay down their lives for Christ and be a thriving member of our church family, they need to have a healthy view of the church.

THE MOSES GENERATION

I learned the importance of vision one day after comparing and contrasting the differences between Moses' generation and Joshua's generation. The story of Joshua captured my heart. Joshua is on the brink of leading Israel into the Promised Land. After forty years of wandering, God lifts the ban and began to prepare Joshua's generation to go into the Promised Land. Forty years earlier, the leaders of Moses' generation decided not to trust God, but choose safety and comfort over obedience and faithfulness.

Remember, forty years earlier, on the brink of entering the Promised Land, Moses gathered twelve leaders—one representing each tribe—to go in and spy out the land. The trip had a two-fold purpose. First, the leaders were to find out if the land was flowing with milk and honey. Second, the leaders should determine what type of enemies they would have to go up against in order to inhabit the land. So the spies went for forty days, and upon their return they came back with their findings.

The report back was astonishing. They announced that the land was everything that God said it would be. They illustrated this by showing the fruit they brought back from the land. However, they also reported that the land is inhabited with giants that would certainly kill them.

The Moses generation, listening to their leaders, determined that it wasn't a good idea to go into the land; instead they chose comfort and safety—except for Joshua and Caleb.

In His anger, God chose to punish Israel. He made a declaration that anyone over the age of twenty would not enter into the Promised Land. And Joshua and Caleb were the only two over the age of twenty that would be allowed to enter into the Promised Land.

THE JOSHUA GENERATION

Fast-forward forty years later. The unfaithful generation who would not trust God is dead—except for Joshua and Caleb. Now Joshua is tasked with the responsibility to rally a generation of believers to give their whole lives to something their parents were unwilling to do. Fear gripped them. Doubt consumed them.

Joshua, however, must have been eager—eager to execute the vision God gave the people forty years ago. The once-young leader, now elder Joshua was confirmed as Israel's leader to lead the people into the Promised Land. The land was still flowing with milk and honey, and still inhabited with giants who hated Israel.

After being instructed to be strong and courageous, Joshua leads his people over the Jordan to the outskirts of Jericho, the first city to conquer. The strategy God gives Joshua is fascinating. The instructions were for seven days, every day, one time per day, walk around the city and sing praises to their God, Yahweh. They were to do this every day for seven days. And on the seventh day, they were to walk around Jericho seven times. And on the seventh day, God told Joshua He would make all the walls come down and then the army could charge the city.

For Joshua, a studied military expert, this plan did not seem strategic or realistic. But God had a bigger point to accomplish. He wanted to paint a picture to Joshua's generation that the battle is not theirs. The battle belongs to the Lord. Success is found in faithfulness and obedience to Him as their King.

Unlike their parents, the Joshua generation did exactly what God called them to do. And God was faithful to do exactly what He told them He would do.

Have you ever compared and contrasted these two generations?

Moses' generation was unwilling to go because they focused on an anti-vision. Joshua's generation was willing to go because not only did they have vision, they were willing to trust God to accomplish this vision.

Remember: People give their time, talent, and treasure to vision, and people give their time, talent, and treasure to being specifically asked to give.

Isn't that an amazing story? I remember hearing and being captured by that story for the first time as a student at the University of North Texas. I was determined to be obedient to God's Word (no matter the consequences), so I gathered my believing friends in the dormitory hallway and cast a vision to them and asked them to help me carry out a specific vision.

I retold the story of Joshua to those who gathered that night. And I told them the plan was for us to do exactly what the Joshua generation did. Although we did not have a physical war, we had a spiritual one. Although we did not fight against flesh and blood, we fought against spirits and principalities. Although we didn't have a city to conquer, we had a club to save. So the plan was simple: we were going to identify the most popular nightclub in the area, but instead of walking around the club for seven days, we were going to gather in front of the club and pray. While the literal walls of the club may not come down, we fully believed and trusted God that the walls of people's hearts would come down—that they would come running out with a desire to trust Jesus as their Lord and Savior.

That night, we lined up at the entrance of the club with our hearts pounding and excitement running through our veins. We prayed passionately with expectant hearts. That night, no one actually came and asked, "What must I do to be saved?" Instead, the police pulled up and told us we couldn't do this. We were breaking the law and we were on private property. Unwavering about the fact we were in God's will, everyone left rejoicing because we were persecuted for our faith!

Was this whole expedition foolish? Probably so.

Would I do this now? Probably not!

However, I realized one thing as I reflected on that night. People give their time, talent, and treasure to vision, and people give their time, talent, and treasure to being specifically asked to give.

THE ANTI-VISION

Unfortunately, the church is known more for what we are *against* than what we are *for*. If you are like me, early in your Christian walk you were mostly told all the things you needed to change in your life in order to be a faithful Christian. No one talked to me about all the things God actually wants me to do for Him as a wise steward. I was very clear on the vision of what *not* to do (anti-vision); however, I was unsure and uncertain of what God was calling me *to* do (vision).

THE VISION

When I finally realized that God was not simply calling us to stop doing things but He was also calling us to start doing things, my walk with Christ changed dramatically. After attending several different Bible studies, I was introduced to new terms that I had not yet learned in my early walk with Christ. These new terms were *evangelism* and *discipleship*. Although I knew my friends loved the Lord, their Christianity was marked by an anti-vision, not a proactive vision.

Yes, God is calling us away from some things. But, He is also calling us *to* some things. What I learned was my friends' emphasis, negativity toward sin, in their walk with Christ was not wrong; it was just incomplete: "Submit yourselves therefore to God. Resist the devil, and he will flee from you. Draw near to God, and he will draw near to you" (James 4:7–8). God is calling us to both resist and submit. We are to manage all of our time, talent, and treasure, as resources, not to run *from* something, but to run *to* something: Christ's vision!

CHRIST'S VISION

In the next significant movement in the book of Matthew, Jesus gathers His disciples to inaugurate the next season of ministry. Up to this point, there have been a lot of peaks and valleys in the ministry of Christ and His disciples. As resistance mounts, Jesus calls His disciples away for retreat in order to cast a clear and compelling vision. Let's look at the text,

> Now when Jesus came into the district of Caesarea Philippi, he asked his disciples, "Who do people say that the Son of Man is?" And they said, "Some say John the Baptist, others say Elijah, and others Jeremiah or one of the prophets." He said to them, "But who do you say that I am?" Simon Peter replied, "You are the Christ, the Son of the living God." And Jesus answered him, "Blessed are you, Simon Bar-Jonah! For flesh and blood has not revealed this to you, but my Father who is in heaven. And I tell you, you are Peter, and on this rock I will build my church, and the gates of hell shall not prevail against it. I will give you the keys of the kingdom of heaven, and whatever you bind on earth shall be bound in heaven, and whatever you loose on earth shall be loosed in heaven." Then he strictly charged the disciples to tell no one that he was the Christ.
>
> From that time Jesus began to show his disciples that he must go to Jerusalem and suffer many things from the elders and chief priests and scribes, and be killed, and on the third day be raised. And Peter took him aside and began to rebuke him, saying, "Far be it from you, Lord! This shall never happen to you." But he turned and said to Peter, "Get behind me, Satan! You

are a hindrance to me. For you are not setting your mind on the things of God, but on the things of man." Then Jesus told his disciples, "If anyone would come after me, let him deny himself and take up his cross and follow me." (Matt. 16:13–24)

Let's take a brief look at the clear and compelling vision Christ gives to His disciples. Below are the five components:

1. Clarity of and Commitment to the Person of Christ
2. Clarity of and Commitment to the People of Christ
3. Clarity of and Commitment to the Mission
4. Clarity of and Commitment to the Gathering
5. Clarity of and Commitment to the Cost

CLARITY OF AND COMMITMENT TO THE PERSON OF CHRIST

Jesus takes His disciples to Caesarea Philippi, and the first thing He seeks to bring clarity to is who He is and what He has come to do. Jesus asked His disciples, "Who do people say that I am?"

If you notice, the answers given are all over the map.

As Jesus' disciples today, we need to answer the same question: "Who do you say that He is?" In this passage we see that the "You" is both emphatic and plural, meaning that the answer to this question was important for the disciples to know, and this was something Jesus expects all His disciples to know. Peter, being the spokesman of the group, stood up and said, "You are the Christ the son of the living God." Stating His full name (like your parents do when something is important), Jesus affirms his confession. Jesus then takes it a step further and reveals His vision in light of Him being the Son of God: "I will build my church."

If we are going to have a clear understanding of Jesus' vision, we must first be clear on who Jesus is. He is the Christ, the Son of the living God. This clearly separates him from any other man, religious or not. If we are going to gather the people around a vision, we must first be clear on who it is we are actually rallying around.

CLARITY OF AND COMMITMENT TO THE PEOPLE OF CHRIST

As stated earlier, the church is not *like* family, it *is* a family in which God is our Father, Jesus is our older brother, and we are brothers and sisters in Christ. Therefore, if we are in Christ and He is our older brother, all believers both locally and globally are brothers and sisters in Christ. Often, we are comfortable making a commitment to Jesus, but we are even more uncomfortable making a commitment to His people.

Let's look at these words again, "upon this rock I will build my church." The key word for us to unearth in the sentence is the word "church." On one end of the spectrum, some believe "I am the church. Wherever I go, I am the church because Christ is in me." On the other end of the spectrum, some blindly follow leaders, perhaps a Pope-like figure, who intercedes on their behalf. Although, as Protestants, we don't call them the Pope. Instead, we use terms like "the man of God." And we determine that we cannot hear from God and His Word on our own, so we must first go to them in order for us to clearly hear from Him. Both of these caricatures are wrong.

Church is not a commonly used word in the Gospels. In fact, it is only used twice. Both appearances occur in the book of Matthew—first in Matthew 16:18, and second in Matthew 18:17. The core of the meaning of the word is "a called-out group of people." Not an event, or an individual, or a Sunday service, or a conference, or a concert. The church is a group of people, called out by Christ (*not* the place we go to on Sundays).

The word *church* is mentioned more than one hundred times in the remaining books of the New Testament. Contrary to popular opinion, when referring to the church, the Bible refers more commonly to the local, tangible church than the universal and intangible church. The local church is where we are able to make an abstract gospel concrete. Mark Dever rightly says that the "local church is the gospel made visible."[40]

So what exactly was Jesus doing when He cast vision to His disciples about gathering His people? Right after the declaration that Jesus is the Son of God, He builds upon this reality. He basically tells them that He is the Son of God and He is gathering a group of people.

But the question is, *Why* is Christ gathering His disciples?

CLARITY OF AND COMMITMENT TO THE MISSION

After solidifying that a commitment to Him is a commitment to His family (i.e., the church), Jesus gives the reason why He is gathering His people. His vision for the mission is clear: "God is mobilizing an army to attack the gates of hell!"

"And I tell you, you are Peter, and on this rock I will build my church, and the gates of hell shall not prevail against it." (Matt. 16:18)

If you look carefully at this verse, one of the things you see is that the church is meant to be on the offensive, not the defensive. Gates are a defensive mechanism in the midst of war. When an enemy approaches, all of the farmers retreat to the city gates. As the enemy comes near, they do everything they can to keep them outside the gates because the enemy knows, if they can get on the inside the gates, the people are vulnerable and most easily defeated.

This is what we saw in the story of Joshua. This is what we see now. Jesus did not call His disciples to build the church and then put up gates to keep hell at bay. The church is not a city under siege, as if hell was fast approaching and we need to keep it out. Jesus says the absolute opposite. Jesus is building a church that is going to mobilize as an army to attack the darkness of hell, and no fortress or gates are going to stop it!

The problem is most of our churches are not mobilized to attack the gates of hell. Instead, they are built as fortresses in order to keep hell out of the church. This is where we primarily see anti-vision instead of a vision. Unfortunately, we are more known for what we are against then what we are for. We are more focused on fleeing temptation than pursuing righteousness.

However, if people give their time, talent, and treasure to vision, we have to give our people a complete vision—not just to flee sin but to pursue righteousness. We must provide a clear and compelling vision for mission. Otherwise, like the Moses generation, our generation is prone to chose comfort and safety over trust and faithfulness.

CLARITY OF AND COMMITMENT TO THE GATHERING

Rallying people around Christ's mission can seem daunting. One of the reasons is that most believers have no desire to be on mission for Christ. Second, the ones who do want to be on mission often have their own agenda. So if you have any experience trying to rally people around a specific vision in regards to mission, you have realized this task is like trying to herd cats! Many denominations have been birthed from the belief that we can do more together than apart. The question for this generation is, do we still believe that?

> "I will give you the keys of the kingdom of heaven, and whatever you bind on earth shall be bound in heaven, and whatever you loose on earth shall be loosed in heaven." Then he strictly charged the disciples to tell no one that he was the Christ." (Matt. 16:19–20)

All authority is given to *we*, not *me*!

Christ, understanding this hardship, gives a unique authority to the gathered church.

This authority to bind and loose is not given to an individual; it is given to the local church.

I understand we face a complexity of problems due to the density and diversity of our cities. I also understand that there is not one church or one mission that will accomplish all the needs of a particular neighborhood or city. However, I do believe we need to provide more unity, not uniformity, in our mission.

Uniformity is a group of people pursuing a common purpose with only one strategy. This is when a person thinks that unity is assimilation, where the goal is to make look-a-likes of whomever the strongest or most prominent person in the room is. Uniformity kills true diversity in the body because it reinforces parroting, inauthenticity, and outward conformity.

Unity, on the other hand, is a group of people banding together for a common purpose, in their own unique strategies. Unity looks like a football team. You have a group of people with different positions and different responsibilities, but they are all trying to achieve the same goal. And that goal is what drives them. In unity, there is dignity, empowerment, and trust.

The key difference between the two is that uniformity shrinks the beauty of our complexities, and shrinks it to simple outward conformity. Unity reinforces mutual solidarity—rallying us around a common vision and goal.

Remember, God has gifted us uniquely for the common good. But oftentimes, like the world, we are unable to work together for God's common vision. We must ask ourselves, especially in the urban context, is our mission ultimately to fulfill God's purpose or to get our fame within God's purposes?

I have firsthand experience when it comes to this hardship. I am part of a band of brothers with a unique burden to be the last generation of minorities to leave the urban context in search of sound discipleship. What started off as a clear vision to bring the message of the person and work of Christ into every neighborhood, what started as an attempt to establish a tangible presence of that message in our cities, has turned into a quest for comfort and a desire to grab bigger platforms of greater influence. This shift tears at the fabric of corporate unity, hindered our ability to be God's gathered people locally.

The ability to stay together in unity is not an easy task. If you don't believe me, ask Kobe and Shaq, the former big three in Miami (LeBron, Wade, and Bosh), or any other great sports dynasty. There are always things pulling at the fabric of unity, whether it's ambition, pride, or a lack of contentment. Our ability to stay together as a picture of reconciliation in the church is a demonstration of the power of God.

Therefore we must fight for unity, as God's people.

CLARITY OF AND COMMITMENT TO THE COST

> From that time Jesus began to show his disciples that he must go to Jerusalem and suffer many things from the elders and chief priests and scribes, and be killed, and on the third day be raised. And Peter took him aside and began to rebuke him, saying, "Far be it from you, Lord! This shall never happen to you." But he turned and said to Peter, "Get behind me, Satan! You are a hindrance to me. For you are not setting your mind on the things of God, but on the things of man." Then Jesus told his disciples, "If anyone would come after me, let him deny himself and take up his cross and follow me." (Matt. 16:21–24)

Fresh off the heels of making probably the greatest statement he has made, Peter makes one of the greatest mistakes he will make. Here's what I imagine the conversation sounding like:

Jesus: All right all right, gather around. So some people say that I am John the Baptist, some say Elijah, some say just a prophet. Okay, who do you say that I am?

Peter: You are the Christ, the Son of the living God.

Jesus: Peter, you're right. And upon the fact that I am the Son of God, I am gathering a group of people to attack the gates of hell.

<disciples cheer>

Jesus: Not only that, I am going to give this gathered people that you meet authority if they remain together.

<disciples cheer, after they settle down, Jesus continues>

Jesus: Okay, here's the plan. I must go back to Jerusalem, and I'm going to die.

<cheering immediately stops, Jesus dampened the mood. Peter (being the bold one who says what everybody else is thinking, especially after the homerun he hit with his last confession) pulls Jesus aside.>

Peter: Jesus, this is not a good plan!

The disciples are excited because they are gaining momentum; their movement is growing in strength. But they are utterly confused. Jesus just said His plan was to die!

Jesus, seizing this as a teachable moment, seeks to clarify both the vision and the call to commitment from His followers.

Jesus tells Peter, "Get behind me, Satan." He lets Peter know that he is thinking like the world, thinking that the goal of life is self-preservation. Jesus is saying, "I must go back to Jerusalem and die. And in fact, if anyone wants to follow after Me, they also must die, deny themselves, take up their cross and follow Me."

Jesus paints a very clear picture of what is about to take place in a very specific call to what it means to follow Him. How many of us who are seeking to establish a tangible presence in our neighborhoods or city are calling people to die? Instead, we are often calling people to a better life now.

Jesus wants to make it crystal clear that the call to disciple-making is a call to *die*!

If we are going to call people to vision and, specifically, call people to giving their time, talent, and treasure to the specific vision, then the vision for corporate mission must be worthy not only to die for, but also to live for.

This vision must establish clarity on the person of Christ, the people of Christ, the mission of Christ, the authority we have in Christ, and ultimately count the cost of following Christ!

CHAPTER 11

MOVEMENT #8: UNLEASHING DISCIPLE-MAKERS

THE WORDS MY DAD SAID TO ME WHEN I WAS SIX YEARS OLD will never leave me. He said, "Son, you have a God-given talent."

At the time, I did not know what that meant, but I remember the time so vividly. I just finished playing my first tackle football game at Joe Brown Park in New Orleans. I had a good game. I scored multiple touchdowns and clearly demonstrated that I had some natural talent—just like my dad. Those words were all I needed. For better or worse, it shaped my identity for years to come. Football became my North Star. The identity I found in it shaped every aspect of my life. I doubt my dad knew how significant those words would be to me.

People oftentimes don't realize how impactful their words can be. We grow up hearing the lie that words will never hurt us. However, Jesus knows how important words are. Well-placed words can be life-shaping. The words Jesus states in Matthew 28:18–20 are both life-shaping and life-giving.

And Jesus came and said to them, "All authority in heaven and on earth has been given to me. Go therefore and *make disciples* of all nations, baptizing them in the name of the Father and of the Son and of the Holy Spirit, teaching them to observe all that I have commanded you. And behold, I am with you always, to the end of the age." (Matt. 28:18–20, emphasis added)

These words help many people get incredibly focused on the mission God has called us to. These words also haunt people who turn Jesus' words from the Great Commission into a mild suggestion. But, these words clearly give us marching orders to make disciples. This is why I believe disciple-making is not a ministry of the church; it is *the* ministry of the church.

Disciple-making is the vision God has for His people.

Disciple-making is bringing people into God's family.

Disciple-making is why any of us enter into ministry.

Disciple-making is what we are calling people to commit to.

Disciple-making is the work of the laborer.

Disciple-making is how we are trained.

Disciple-making is why we are mobilized corporately.

Disciple-making is not a mild suggestion.

Disciple-making is the Great Commission.

The first movement in Matthew began with God the Father bestowing authority on Jesus. This final movement ends in the same way. In the first movement, God intertwines His story with Joseph's story and gives him a unique burden to establish God's presence among us. In the second movement, God breaks four hundred years of silence with the announcement of His Son Jesus, who will establish His family. In movement 3, as Jesus enters into ministry, He overcomes the temptations to take the easy way out and presses onward in the difficult entrance into ministry. In movement 4, Jesus preached a new reality for God's covenant family, calling people to repentance. In movement 5, He calls His disciples to labor with Him in making disciples.

In movement 6, He trains them. In movement 7, He mobilizes them to attack the gates of hell. And in Matthew 28, we see Jesus giving His final words to make disciples.

Within the Great Commission, there is one imperative and three participles describing how to fulfill the imperative. The one imperative is to make disciples. The supporting participles explain *how* we are to make disciples: going, baptizing, and teaching. How you view these three participles will shape how you approach disciple-making.

ALL AUTHORITY

At the beginning and end of the Great Commission, Christ declares His lordship and challenges us to place Him in a place of preeminence in our lives. Jesus says all authority has been given to Him. It's a claim to who He is. He goes on and says we are to "observe all I have commanded you." He ends with the promise, "I am with you always." He has all authority, He tells us to obey all He has commanded us, and, finally, He promises to always be with us.

These three things shape the preeminence of who Christ is. Understanding who Christ is, is critical to our understanding of who we are. These verses serve as a reminder that all authority has been given to Christ. It tells us He has given us a real commission to go and make disciples. ALL authority, not partial or some, but all authority belongs to Christ. This is a call for Christ's preeminence—not prominence—in your life. Many of us have Christ as prominent but not preeminent. Prominence in our life might look like the statement, "I put God first, then my wife, kids, and family." But Jesus is after more than that. He is saying He demands a place of preeminence. Think of it this way. If I were to say I'm married to Angie and she's my #1 girl, but you know I've got my #2 and #3 girls over here. Would anyone be impressed that I put Angie as #1? No, of course not. It's not impressive. That's why the Scripture says that if you want to follow Christ, you have to hate your mother and father and brothers and sisters. Christ is asking for a place of preeminence. He is saying, "Compared to Me and My sovereign will, everything else should pale in comparison."

This is why the beginning of wisdom is the fear of the Lord. The fear of the Lord is a place of reverence and preeminence where we are so consumed and concerned with how He thinks that it shapes and guides everything in our lives.

Many of us need to recalibrate our hearts. Is Christ really Lord of your life? For some of you, He may be a great Savior. But is He the reigning Lord?

For others of you, He might be helpful to keep you out of hell. But, is He helpful in your day-to-day? Is He supreme over each moment?

Before we can move onto the commands of the Great Commission, we must understand the place of preeminence demanded and deserved by Jesus Christ. And if Christ is Lord, we are His servants, His bond-servants. And that identity radically reshapes our lives and impacts what we do. We see what Jesus commands in the Great Commission and our whole lives reshape around a goal to see it accomplished. But that activity comes out of our identity as servants of the Lord.

Not only is it critical for us to recognize the authority of the One who gave us the Great Commission, we need to understand the gravity of the commission, itself. We've taken the Great Commission and turned it into a mild suggestion. We act as if it is up to us to decide if we want to do what God has called us to do, as if we get to decide if we feel like being his witnesses. We fail to understand the weight of the imperative. Finally, we need to prioritize our lives in a way to fulfill it. All authority has been given to Him. He has called us to make disciples. Therefore, we must reorganize our lives to achieve that end.

GO MAKE DISCIPLES OF ALL NATIONS

How you interpret the first part of this text is critical. Some believe "going" is the most important part of the Great Commission. The different ways people interpret this first verb impacts the process of disciple-making. Some take the "go" to mean "go right now," while some like to take a more casual "as you are going" approach. The interpretation of this participle has been used to guilt some believers to start laboring for the harvest, while others have used it as an excuse to keep our normal self-centered routine with just a little sprinkle of Christ in it. While both of these are caricatures, they illustrate the different ways well-intentioned leaders have tried to motivate Christ followers to do what God has clearly called us to. Therefore, I would like to introduce a third way to interpret this first verb.

Dr. Daniel B. Wallace, executive director of the Center for the Study of New Testament Manuscripts and senior professor of New Testament Studies at Dallas Theological Seminary, writes,

> It is true that the word translated "go" is a participle. But it is not a present participle, which is the one that would be required if the meaning were "as you are going." It is an aorist participle, πορευθέντες (*poreuthentes*). As such, it hardly means "as you are going" or "while you are going." The basic idea would be "after you have gone," and as such would presuppose that one would have gone forth before making disciples.[41]

Oftentimes, I believe we are not asking the same questions the Bible is asking. I don't believe Jesus is splitting hairs on the force of "the go." I think He makes the assumption that disciples are following Him, so they are already going. I believe Jesus wished to emphasize that as those who have already gone, we should be making disciples.

Because we don't know what it means to actually follow Christ, we don't know what it means to truly be sent. Paul says it like this in 1 Corinthians 9:16–17, "For if I preach the gospel, that gives me no ground for boasting. For necessity is laid upon me. Woe to me if I do not preach the gospel! For if I do this of my own will, I have a reward, but if not of my own will, I am still entrusted with a stewardship." Paul believes the wrestle is not with the manner in which we are going, because the assumption of a disciple is that you have already gone. You are entrusted with stewardship of the gospel.

Let me illustrate this for you in the life of Paul. Wherever Paul was, he understood he was sent. If Paul was shipwrecked, then those people who worked with him were coming to know the Lord. If Paul was put in prison, then prisoners were coming to know the Lord. If Paul was put in the university town, then the students and professors would be hearing the gospel. Why? Because "going" for Paul was not something he did—it was who he was. He was sent by the Lord.

I believe this is critical for us who are laboring among wolves because God has brought the nations to our front door. We need to move from an ethnic missiology to a neighbor missiology. Through urbanization, God has brought the nations to our front doorsteps, to our neighborhoods, where we live, where we work, and where we play. Let's assume we have been sent. We are the sent-ones of God.

Therefore, "Go—make disciples."

BAPTIZING THEM

The question may be asked, "Why should we assume we have gone?" But then comes in the second verb, *baptizing*. The process of baptizing is as much about adopting our new identity as it is the activity of being placed under water. You have likely heard the phrase, "Sticks and stones will break my bones but words will never hurt me." This is an English-language children's rhyme that is reported to have appeared in the *Christian Recorder* in March of 1862. It was a way for parents to equip their children to deal with name-calling and refrain from physical retaliation. Growing up, it was a saying that used to help us cope with the harsh words people said about us.

Looking back over your childhood, did you believe this rhyme? How many of you were called an Uncle Tom? Sellout? Oreo? Tomboy? White trash? Stuck-up? Goody Two-Shoes? Know-it-all? And how much have these words shaped your identity even to this day? Why is it that we believe the negative things said about us more easily than we believe the positive things? Why do we more readily identify with the things that bring division than those that bring us together?

First Corinthians 15:33 states, "Do not be deceived: 'Bad company ruins good morals.'" And for many of us, this bad company, or at least the bad words, have formed our identities today. This is why this word *baptized* is important for us to understand in shaping our identity in Christ. Identity drives our activity, and our activities reinforce our identity. Another way to say it is: who we are drives what we do, and what we do reinforces who we are.

Baptism declares our new identity in Christ. We are a new creation. Let's revisit Matthew 28:18–20, "And Jesus came and said to them, 'All authority in heaven and on earth has been given to me. Go therefore and make disciples of all nations, baptizing them in the name of the Father and of the Son and of the Holy Spirit, teaching them to observe all that I have commanded you. And behold, I am with you always, to the end of the age.'" This commission begins with the identity of the One who has all authority. This is Jesus. The significance of Jesus having all authority is critical. Matthew is establishing the preeminence of Christ in our culture. He establishes that He has all authority, then calls us to observe all He has commanded, and then tells us He will always be with us.

How we view Christ will impact how we live our lives. Jeff Vanderstelt, in his book *Saturate*, believes gospel fluency promotes gospel identity.[42] The more we fully understand the person and work of Christ, the more we truly understand who we are and what we've been called to. I believe this is significant, especially as we are to make disciples of all nations. If we are coming from many different nations to become a new creation in Christ Jesus, we must be willing to lay down our identities that have been formed by our different nations and take on the new identity of being in Christ. This is very important for those of us ministering in urban contexts, as we strive for harmony in the dense and diverse chaos that cities bring.

I learned this in a significant way through marrying my wife. My wife and I came from two different cultures. We had a common union with the person and work of Christ and a preeminent view that His ways were above our ways. However, our different cultural understandings and practices created a great rub in day-to-day life as a newly married couple. After just three months of being married, we were already back in the counselor's room, desperate for solutions to the problems we had.

The advice we got was a significant push for us to strive after our new identity in Christ. We understood that if we were to become more Christlike, we needed to be willing to lay down our lives in order to find a new one together. In the process, I did not become any less black and Angie did not become any less white. We became two new creations with newfound identities in Christ. And this newfound identity was marked first and foremost by love.

Baptism is commanded by Jesus (Matt. 28:19) and the apostles (Acts 2:38). Therefore, it is necessary if we are to be obedient to Christ. Baptism is to our identity in Christ, as my wedding ring symbolizes my covenant marriage to Angela. A wedding ring does not make a person married, but it indicates that a marriage has taken place. Baptism is not a condition of salvation, but it declares our new union with and identity in Christ.

TEACHING TO OBSERVE ALL THAT
I HAVE COMMANDED

What does it mean to observe all that He has commanded? We don't have to look far because Jesus stated earlier in Matthew 22:37 that all the commandments hang on two commands: that we love the Lord God with all our heart, mind, soul, and strength, and that we love our neighbors as much as we love ourselves. So what it means to teach to the point of obedience is to teach another to fall more in love with God and more in love with one another. Paul states, "But the goal of our instruction is love from a pure heart and a good conscience and a sincere faith" (1 Tim. 1:5 NASB). God is calling us to live by the Great Commandment as we live out the Great Commission.

Christianity is simple in its message, but supernatural in its application. The reason it's hard to live authentically Christian in the urban context is because we are called to supernaturally love those who don't look like us, talk like us, or act like us. We are called to love those who don't get us. This is why we desperately need God's presence through the Holy Spirit to do the very things that we want to do, but find ourselves unable to do. It's one thing for us to know that we are called to love; it's another thing to have the power to love.

CONCLUSION: I WILL BE WITH YOU

Matthew ends his gospel in the same way he began, with the promise of presence. As one of my mentors, Dr. Crawford Loritts, often says, "Ninety percent of ministry is just showing up."[43] My prayer as we embrace the call to labor among wolves is that we would commit to continually show up. And then we would trust in the person and work of Christ and the power of His Spirit to do the rest!

The Great Commission calls us to make disciples as followers of Christ. We do this in our jobs, our homes, and our neighborhoods—all with the goal of subduing them and recapturing those arenas as vital gospel ground. And as you go into those places, baptize, teach, and live out your new identity in Christ.

I pray that as you wrestle with the totality of the Great Commission, that as you feel conviction, you also feel rest. Yes, we are ministering *among wolves*, but our God is Lord of the harvest. We should be challenged to submit to His authority, but we can also rest in His sovereignty and the promise of His presence. When He says, "Go therefore and make disciples and I will always be with you," He is going back to every movement.

- In movement 1, God says all these things took place so that Jesus could be with us. (IMMANUEL)
- In movement 2, God shows how the Father is supernaturally with the Son in baptism through a descending dove, an audible voice, and the confirmation of John the Baptist.
- In movement 3, the Holy Spirit led Jesus into the wilderness and, after the third temptation, Jesus is met with a multitude of angels surrounding Him.
- In movement 4, Jesus calls His disciples to be with Him.
- In movement 5, we see the grievous situation of sheep without a shepherd and the call for the disciples to labor among the harvest—to shepherd the lost sheep.
- In movement 6, Jesus challenges His disciples not to send off the crowds but to feed them and be with them.
- In movement 7 in Matthew 16, Jesus asks, "Who do you say that I am?" Peter responds, "You're the Son of God." And Jesus says, "You're right. And on this fact, I am gathering a group of people to attack the gates of hell together, with one another."

- And finally, in movement 8, Jesus declares His preeminent authority and commands us to make disciples as we go, baptizing, teaching, and clinging onto His presence.

AFTERWORD

TAKE HEART—TAKE ON THE WORLD

BY JORGE MENDOZA

THERE IS NO ONE I TRUST AND RESPECT MORE THAN DHATI Lewis when it comes to living on mission and everyday discipleship. We have been friends, neighbors, and co-laborers. I've been able to observe firsthand the kind of impact from living out the principles you have read about in *Among Wolves*. I'm honored to add a concluding thought to Dhati's insightful work on Matthew's Gospel.

In the Gospel of Matthew we not only have a reliable testimony to the life and message of Jesus, we also have a literary work of art. The more you examine it, the more beauty you unearth. For example, if you step back and look at the Gospel of Matthew as a whole, you would notice that he concludes his account with a theme that was present at the beginning, a promise of the divine presence. These two promises are twin pillars to encourage our hearts in life and mission.

In Matthew 1:23 the angel announces the birth of Christ saying: "'Behold, the virgin shall conceive and bear a son, and they shall call his name Immanuel' (which means, God with us)." In Matthew 28:20, the resurrected Christ says to His disciples, "Behold, I am with you always, to the end of the age."

These promises are similar in essence but distinct in purpose. They both present the same ineffable reality that the divine presence is with us but they are meant to produce two different but complementary results. The context of each promise helps us to grasp the distinction.

In chapter 1 the promise of the presence appears in the context of Christ coming into the world as the angel announces the birth of Christ. He is coming to redeem us. In chapter 28, the promise of the presence is in the context of Christ departing from the world. He has conquered death and is now at the point of His ascension to reign. In chapter 1 God desires to do something for us—forgive our sins (v. 21). In chapter 28, God desires to do something through us—make disciples of the nations (v. 19).

Like pushing on the two pedals of a bicycle keeps us stable and moving forward, believing these two promises does the same for our hearts and lives. The first promise stabilizes our hearts in a secure relationship with the Father, "God is with us." The second promise keeps us moving forward in mission by assuring us that we will have His help in the task, "Go . . . I will be with you!"

The first promise is there to comfort us; the second is there to compel us. The first promise invites us in; the second pushes us out. The first promise shows love to us; the second shows love to others. The first promise assures forgiveness for us; the second announces forgiveness for others. The first promise welcomes us to know His glorious person; the second strengthens to fulfill His global purpose. The first promise encourages us to take heart; the second promise encourages us to take on the world!

So as the Lord Jesus sends you out *among wolves*, He does not send you alone. He is with you.

NOTES

1. Mark Gottdiener and Ray Hutchinson, *The New Urban Sociology* (Boulder: Westview Press, 2010), 15.

2. Ibid., 44.

3. Values and Research Institute, https://www.namb.net/send-cities/newyorkcity/.

4. Gottdiener and Hutchinson, *The New Urban Sociology*, 14.

5. Ibid., 17.

6. CNN Correspondent Ann Chu, Thursday, March 11, 2004, Posted: 7:53 p.m. EST.

7. Benjamin Meadows Ingram, *Vibe Magazine*, 2002.

8. S. Mackinnon, C. Jordan, and A. Wilson, "Birds of a Feather Sit Together: Physical Similarity Predicts Seating Choice," *Personality and Social Psychology Bulletin, 37* (2011), 7.

9. Ibid., 212.

10. Adi Joseph, *USA TODAY*, Sports 8:43 a.m. EDT, May 23, 2014.

11. Margaret Severance, *Official Guide to Atlanta: Including Information of the Cotton States and International Exposition* (Atlanta, GA: Foote & Davies Co., 1895), 42. Retrieved 2011-01-02.

12. Scott Henry, "Down on Boulevard: Positive Change Might Finally Come to Atlanta's Lawless Street," *Creative Loafing Atlanta* (May 19, 2009). Retrieved 2009-06-06.

13. Hendricks Howard, see http://seacoast-church.org/howard-hendricks-quotes/.

14. Henry T. Blackaby and Richard Blackaby, *Spiritual Leadership: Moving People on to God's Agenda* (Nashville, TN: Broadman & Holman Publishers, 2001), 103.

15. Source unknown.

16. Dr. Edwards, Gang Historian, as quoted in, "If the Streets of Atlanta Could Talk, Atlanta Part 1," https://www.youtube.com/watch?v=pTXqi-zAgsE.

17. Michael Goheen, *A Light to the Nations: The Missional Church and the Biblical Story* (Grand Rapids, MI: Baker Academic, 2011), 6.

18. Wilbert R. Shenk, foreword to *Images of the Church in Mission* by John Driver (Scottsdale, PA: Herald Press, 1997), 9, as cited in Goheen, *A Light to the Nations*, 6.

19. Paul Minear, *Images of the Church in the New Testament* (Louisville, KY: John Knox Press, 2004), 268–69.

20. Joseph Hellerman, *When the Church Was a Family: Recapturing Jesus' Vision for Authentic Christian Community* (Nashville, TN: B&H Publishing, 2009), 121.

21. Ibid.

22. Carmen Solomon-Fears, Gene Falk, and Adrienne L. Fernandes-Alcantara, "Child Well-Being and Noncustodial Fathers," *Congressional Research Service*, 7-5700 (Feb. 12, 2013), 6, https://www.fas.org/sgp/crs/misc/R41431.pdf.

23. Ibid., 14.

24. Ibid., 2–3.

25. George Eldon Ladd, *A Theology of the New Testament* (Grand Rapids, MI: Eerdmans, 1993), 109.

26. Mike Breen and Steve Cockram, *Building a Discipling Culture: How to Release a Missional Movement by Discipling People Like Jesus Did* (Pawleys Island, SC: 3 Dimension Ministries, 2011), 20, iBooks.

27. See http://www.desiringgod.org/articles/good-parents-connect-not-just-correct.

28. Max Anders, *30 Days to Understanding the Bible* (Nashville, TN: Thomas Nelson, 2004), 94.

29. *Strong's Exhaustive Concordance of the Bible* (Peabody, MA: Hendrickson Publishers, 2007), 202.

30. John Piper, "Sheep, Wolves, Snakes, and Doves," October 24, 2007, *Desiring God*, http://www.desiringgod.org/articles/sheep -wolves-snakes-and-doves.

31. Elizabeth Shakman Hurd, *Beyond Religious Freedom: The New Global Politics of Religion* (Princeton, NJ: Princeton University Press, 2015), xi.

32. Charles Spurgeon, *The Metropolitan Tabernacle Pulpit: Sermons Preached and Revised by Charles H. Spurgeon during the Year 1876*, Vol. XXII (London: Passmore & Alabaster, 1877), 355, https://books.google.com/books?id=iilOAQAAMAAJ&pg=PA35 5&lpg=PA355&dq=A+sheep+in+the+midst+of+wolves+is+safe+co mpared+to+a+Christian+in+the+midst+of+ungodly+men.%E2%80 %9D&source=bl&ots=hjJp6gTFGc&sig=aXta4ABrcFkq7O6rWyro Mdv-uvU&hl=en&sa=X&ved=0ahUKEwiLkZe87OnOAhXM7yY KHfoyB8UQ6AEIKDAC#v=onepage&q&f=false.

33. Charles H. Spurgeon, *Collected Works*, Vol. 1 (Revelation Insight Publishing Co., 2010), 66, https://books.google.com/books ?id=iWKNCwAAQBAJ&pg=PA66&dq=Charles+Spurgeon+says+it +this+way,+He+who+has+gone+on+to+prepare+heaven+for+us+will +not+leave+us+without+provision+for+the+journey.&hl=en&sa =X&ved=0ahUKEwiN9Lim7enOAhUGqB4KHT-pD_YQ6AEIJz AC#v=onepage&q&f=false.

34. N. T. Wright, "Following Jesus: Biblical Reflections on Discipleship" (Grand Rapids, MI: Eerdmans, 1994), 68, https:// books.google.com/books?id=s-tRAgAAQBAJ&printsec=frontco ver&dq=following+jesus&hl=en&sa=X&ved=0ahUKEwjIyqv47- nOAhXDWh4KHaR7BqoQ6AEIHDAA#v=onepage&q&f=fa lse.

35. Chip Dodd, *The Voice of the Heart: A Call to Full Living* (Nashville, TN: Sage Hill Resources, 2014), 92.

36. Ibid., 107.

37. Darrell W. Robinson, *People Sharing Jesus* (Nashville, TN: Thomas Nelson, 1995), 21–23, as cited in https://bible.org/ illustration/plea-fishing.

38. Author got permission to cite Dr. John Ewart from Southeastern Baptist Theological Seminary for the 95 percent statistic.

39. A. W. Tozer, *The Knowledge of the Holy* (New York, NY: Harper One, 1961), 1, https://books.google.com/books?id=7qMk o7zfcqIC&q=what+comes+into+our+minds#v=onepage&q&f=false.

40. Mark Dever, *The Church: The Gospel Made Visible* (Nashville, TN: B&H Academic, 2012).

41. Daniel B. Wallace, "The Great Commission or the Great Suggestion," February 17, 2014, https://danielbwallace.com /2014/02/17/the-great-commission-or-the-great-suggestion.

42. Jeff Vanderstelt, *Saturate: Being Disciples of Jesus in the Everyday Stuff of Life* (Wheaton, IL: Crossway, 2015), 124.

43. Author got permission to cite Dr. Crawford Lorittis for this quote. It was something he heard him say in a live setting.